John A. Hobbs
The Life and Times of
Music Valley's Visionary

JULIE RICHARDSON

FOREWORD BY: Joe West, Major League Baseball, umpire

John A. Hobbs
The Life and Times of
Music Valley's Visionary

GOLDEN COUNTRY, LLC

For information write:
Golden Country, LLC 1308 5th Street Golden, Colorado 80403

Publisher: Golden Country, LLC
Front Cover Center Photo Credit: Tom Powell
Author Photo: Alana Rothstein
Front cover photo of John A. and Joe West courtesy of Jerry Overcast
All photos courtesy of the Hobbs family unless otherwise noted.

Editor: Mike Towle, Win-Win Words, LLC
Interior Layout: Rebecca Finkel, F + P Graphic Design

Although every precaution has been taken to verify the accuracy
of the information contained herein, the author and publisher assume
no responsibility for any errors or omissions. No liability is assumed for
damages that may result from the use of the information contained within.
The stories contained within this book originated through personal interviews
with John A. Hobbs and are based solely on his personal recollection
and interpretation of events.

ISBN hard cover: 978-0-692-88258-0
ISBN soft cover: 978-0-692-85817-2

Library of Congress Control Number: 2017908399

First Edition

Printed in the United States of America

Acknowledgments

I would like to extend a special thank you to John A. Hobbs for his approval, trust, and belief in me to write his life story. Thank you for the countless hours of time you graciously gave in personal interviews and for your hospitality each time I came to town to work on the book with you and your family.

A nod of tremendous gratitude to Joe Hobbs. I could not have succeeded with this enormous task on my own. You have been such a pillar of support throughout the entire project. Your patient and willing assistance with everything is appreciated and recognized more than you know.

Thank you to the entire Hobbs family for providing me with pictures, personal interviews, stories, articles, maps, insights, and, most importantly, the opportunity to write a book about John A. and record his legacy for generations to come.

I would like to acknowledge Nancy Quinn for her friendship, vote of confidence, and hospitality.

A heartfelt thank you to Marty Martel for introducing me to the special corner with John A. and the gang.

Joe West, I am grateful for your words and willingness to write the foreword for this book. I greatly admire you and your accomplishments and sincerely appreciate your friendship and musical talent.

A very special thank you to all of the dear friends of John A. Hobbs who took the time to interview with me and participate in this very special book with their own stories and personal messages to John A.

Thank you to Steve Sundberg with FTM Studios for preparing and perserving interview audio content.

Most of all, I would like to thank and recognize my mother, Carley Hughes, for her unending patience as I worked through the process of writing this book. You have always been there for me, and I wouldn't be the woman I am today without your love, guidance, and friendship. With all my love and admiration.

—*Julie Richardson*

For John A. Hobbs—

May your legacy live on forever.

For my sons, Joe, Ronnie, Johnny C. and Mike:

without your love, support and help

throughout my life, none of this would be possible.

I love you boys!

Mike, John A., Johnny C., Ronnie, and Joe

Contents

Foreword

The old legend is that if you can count all of your friends on both hands you're a rich man. John A. is therefore the richest man I know. He doesn't have enough hands to count them all.

—JOE WEST, Major League Baseball, umpire

In the mid-1980s, I dabbled in putting out an album, and luckily, I received some national coverage and actually sold a few. So, when I got a call from "Tex" Whitson (Merle Haggard's former manager) telling me that he had me on a show at the Grand Ole Opry, I was excited and thought to myself, "This is great!"

West private collection

The show was a fundraiser for a Catholic Church in Nashville, and I found out later it was being produced by Sam Lovullo. He also produced every taping of *Hee Haw,* the country music variety show. The fundraiser was the idea of a businessman named John A. Hobbs.

When I arrived in Nashville, an old friend of mine, Boxcar Willie, took me under his wing

1

and showed me everywhere around the Opryland Hotel and this big nightclub called The Nashville Palace. I later found out that John A. Hobbs owned The Palace. I can't tell you about my first meeting with Mr. Hobbs because I've promised him I would not "tell all I know." I quickly found out John A. was an avid baseball and Notre Dame fan, and not necessarily in that order. I also found out that he's the reason Boxcar Willie was noticed in Nashville.

Joe Hobbs and John A. reflecting on how far he's come.

He's the reason a lot of others were discovered in Nashville, and he's not the name dropper or person who wants to take any credit for someone being a success. He just wanted to help whomever needed it, and in reading this book you'll see that repeatedly.

He's been a successful businessman because of his work ethic. He's enabled his family to be successful through his vision and sincerity, and he's been a friend to more people than you can count because he's honest to a fault.

I know you'll enjoy reading about a legend because that's what he is. I've often told him that he'll never die, because the Lord doesn't want you, and the devil's afraid you'll take over.

—Joe West

CHAPTER ONE

Most Interesting Person

A life is not important except in the impact it has on other lives.
—JACKIE ROBINSON

I want to be the most interesting eighty-year-old person in the room. Not that I am eighty or anywhere remotely close, but that is the very first line that I wrote on my bucket list. In total, there are one hundred things on the list I chicken-scratched onto a torn and crinkled envelope while flying in a small propeller plane. I had just managed to survive the famous Snowy River Trek in the Australian Outback. I spent a week on horseback, covering forty bone-bruising miles a day, over rugged and unforgiving terrain. I was both exhausted and exhilarated, and I was ready to take on more of what I called living a life of impact.

Upon landing in Sydney, I placed my carefully crafted list, a fail-proof recipe for a life well-lived, in the faded front pocket of my jeans. Slumping back in my seat, I convinced myself that

Julie Richardson, Australian Outback

if I am relentless in my pursuit of the other ninety-nine items, I would undoubtedly be the most interesting person, of any age, in the room.

This was my "truth" until I met John A. Hobbs in Nashville, Tennessee.

John A. Hobbs exudes a light that comes from living a life that enhances the lives of countless others. He is a humble man, fiercely kind with a heart of solid gold. He is also a ferocious and successful businessman with an uncanny vision for the future. John A. is smartly camouflaged in the cloak of an average, everyday man. To glance at him you would never know the extent of his wealth, but you instantly feel his worth to this world to be priceless. His crown, a well-worn and faded Greek fisherman's cap, rests on top of a sharp mind constantly teeming with new ideas. Only those who have spent some time in his corner would even notice the slight movement, back and forth, of his index finger over his lips when he is deep in thought. His wrinkled and calloused hands are strong reminders of the many tasks he has tackled and the many people from all walks of life he has met. John's voice is low, guttural, and gruff; it forces you to lean in and hang on tight to every word of the legendary stories that he tells. They are stories of a life to be revered for the vision and fortitude he showed in creating and guiding the varied and numerous businesses that would shape Music Valley and influence country music. His are anecdotes of gratitude for the opportunities, assistance, and friendships along the way. Those who know him eagerly share his unforgettable acts of kindness and generosity, both slight and voluminous, that impacted their lives.

Anyone fortunate enough to cross paths with this larger-than-life visionary has a different perception and his or her own unique appreciation of him. Having played a vast array of award-winning roles makes John A., well, extremely interesting.

CHAPTER TWO

Entrepreneurs with Vision

*The problems of the world cannot possibly be solved by skeptics
or cynics whose horizons are limited by the obvious realities. We need men
who can dream of things that never were and ask, 'Why not?'*
—JOHN F. KENNEDY

The region known today as Nashville, Tennessee, is no stranger to the likes of John A. Hobbs—entrepreneurs with the vision and audacity to turn a dream into reality. America was founded by men and women with the unyielding determination and gritty strength gained from life's formidable experiences to rise above the most arduous of circumstances and make their own successful path in this life. John A. never set out in life to be rich or famous. He only wanted to better himself and improve his family's situation. Instead of letting adversity derail him, John A. leveraged his most valuable resources—a strong work ethic, charisma, and a talent for engaging people from all backgrounds—so he could make the right connections and stay on track for a life that would make a positive difference for so many. John A.'s life and times epitomize the American Dream, and it has always been about things much simpler and more fundamental than money and stardom: things like lifelong friendships, philanthropy, fairness, gratitude, and service to others.

The foundation of all of humanity, not just in America, is to enhance your circumstances and the lives of those you love. Native American inhabitants thousands of years ago first occupied the area that eventually became Nashville. These Native Americans embraced the fertile land, water, and plentiful hunting grounds this region provided.[1] For years, tribes such as the Shawnee, Cherokee, Creek, and Chickasaw continued to thrive along the life source provided by the Cumberland River.[2]

A wave of European settlers that arrived in the early 1700s included a sharp, French businessman by the name of Jean du Charleville. He was savvy enough to quickly realize the importance of location, starting with construction of a fur trading post near the present-day site of Bicentennial Capitol Mall State Park. The post was strategically placed at a natural sulphur and saline spring. This natural salt lick attracted an abundance of wildlife and consequently, hunters seeking meat and fur. This location, known as the "French Lick," made it convenient and profitable to trade with the local Native Americans.[3] The area's newly booming trade soon caught the attention of Timothy Demonbreun, a French-Canadian fur trapper and entrepreneur who would become known as the "first citizen" of Nashville. With the help of seventeen employees, Demonbreun developed a successful mercantile and fur trading business, and along with that he opened a tavern on Public Square that quickly became popular.[4]

James Robertson and John Donelson arrived near present-day downtown Nashville on Christmas Day 1779. They were surprised and somewhat relieved to encounter Demonbreun, a fellow white man living and prospering in the area. Robertson, a hardy American explorer, Indian agent, and soldier, had left the Watauga settlement in North Carolina and traveled nearly two months overland to reach the vibrant area. Robertson cleared the land, then he built and cofounded Fort Nashborough, named in honor of Francis Nash, an American Revolutionary hero. The community was initially part of the state of North Carolina, and in 1784, the town was officially named Nashville.[5]

With its proximity to several key trading routes, such as the Natchez Trace and the Cumberland River, Nashville soon became a center of commerce, and it rapidly developed. In 1796, North Carolina willingly gave all land from the Allegheny Mountains to the Mississippi River to the federal government. This newly acquired federal territory was admitted to the Union as the state of Tennessee, a name that dates to records from Spanish explorers, who had been to what is now Tennessee in 1567. More than thirty years after its charter, Nashville became the permanent capital of Tennessee in 1843.[6]

The American Civil War, fought from 1861–1865, was the bloodiest internal conflict in American history. The Union withstood secessionists in eleven states, who had banded together as the Confederate States of America. Tennessee was the last state to join the Confederacy in 1861. Only the state of Virginia endured more major battles than Tennessee, resulting in a great deal of destruction throughout cities and farms. As a state capital and strategic shipping port, Nashville quickly became the target of Union forces, culminating in the viciously fought Battle of Nashville in December 1864. Earlier, the Confederate Army had set up fortifications on the south side of the city and managed to hold off

Union forces for a long time before the Battle of Nashville ensued. The heavily outnumbered Confederate forces were defeated and subsequently retreated south to the Tennessee River.

It was far safer in the city than in the rural areas during the war. To sustain fighting, war efforts were needed. Running such war efforts as factories, depots, hospitals, and warehouses produced a strong job market in downtown Nashville, attracting a transient and mixed population of residents. In the wake of the Civil War and with an influx of residents increasing the population, businessmen and entrepreneurs continued to look for money-making opportunities.[7] They eventually succeeded and changed the region's predominantly agricultural economy into one that was industrial and service-oriented. Nashville's population, which had been a mere 345 in 1800, had grown to about ninety thousand Nashvillians by 1900. Today, large numbers of people are still magnetically drawn to the Nashville area—as of 2017 it was growing by about a hundred new arrivals daily—dreaming of a better life and looking to capitalize on the abundant opportunities and resources available.[8]

Only the passage of time and differing circumstances separate John A. Hobbs from these other key figures (Demonbreun, Robertson, etc.) in Nashville's history. Time acts as a powerful sift, leaving behind the nuggets in American history that epitomize the dream. Like his Nashvillian predecessors, John A. Hobbs was born during tumultuous times in America, in his case with the Great Depression and World War II on the horizon. However he developed a clear vision and determination as he plowed his way through life's obstacles, along the way making his mark on American history, much like Demonbreun and Robertson had done years before.

CHAPTER THREE

The Hobbs Family

We all carry inside us people who came before us.
—LIAM CALLANAN, American author

Mary Elizabeth Conroy Hobbs, John A.'s mother, was born November 14, 1903. She was a deeply religious woman with a strong work ethic. She was employed as an all-night chief operator for BellSouth Telephone, where she helped customers place long-distance calls and made sure the switchboard operated smoothly. During the day, Mary labored

as a homemaker; she raised a strong family, made ends meet, and balanced out her husband's destructive habit of drinking with her level-headed and responsible ways.

Mary was brought up in a family of five children; three girls and two boys—

Mary Conroy Hobbs, circa 1990.

Mary Conroy Hobbs, circa 1925.

John Patrick, Martin Joseph, Mary Elizabeth, Nellie Agnes, and
Nora Eugenia. Mary's grandfather, John Conroy, was born in
Ireland in 1831 and, with his wife Bridget, immigrated to the
United States, where he proudly fought for the Confederacy in
the American Civil War. They had two sons together, and their
youngest son was Mary's father, Valentine Cain Conroy, born in
Humphries County in July 1872.

Valentine was a brilliant businessman, land and slave owner, and founder of the first bank in the small town of McEwen, Tennessee. Valentine was considerably older than Mary's mother, Hanoria "Nora" Connally Conroy, whom he married February 1, 1899. He died in 1911 when Mary was just nine years old, leaving behind a small fortune, which Nora smartly invested in a nice three-story house made of brick. It was located at 1404 Natchez Trace Avenue, in a moderately upscale area of Nashville. Nora, the daughter of Irish immigrants, Patrick Connally and Mary Kane Mullen, was born on January 15, 1878 in McEwen, Tennessee. She remarried after Valentine's death and took the last name of McSwiney until her death in 1948 in Nashville. John's father, John Petty Hobbs, was born November 20, 1901, and lived an arduous childhood marked with tragedy. Both of his parents died in their early thirties from apparent kidney problems. Their deaths occurred only a year apart, leaving their young children orphaned. Nine-year-old John Petty, his six-year-old little brother Jim, and baby

Ronnie Hobbs, John Petty Hobbs, and Joe Hobbs, circa 1962.

Emma were left homeless, having to fend for themselves in what is now the Percy Warner Park area.

> Dad reminisced his boyhood with me once in a while, remembering his dad walking down to the spring to fetch water and hollering up for his wife to come down and help him. Dad was just a little one, but he helped his mother carry the water back to the house. The house smelled awful, like something rotted inside, but they didn't know what it was. Unable to afford a doctor back then, everyone simply blamed the deaths on kidney problems.

To survive, the kids were forced to drop out of school early. They drifted from farm to farm, working in exchange for food, shelter, and other basic necessities. Eventually, two elderly bachelor brothers, Willie and Tommy Betts, along with their mother, took the children in and helped raise them.

> Dad shared a story with me one day about his brother Jim and his very first date when he was just eight years old. Jim was headed out the door to walk four country miles to a girl's house for a date. It was wintertime, and there was frost on the ground. They didn't have the money for shoes, and he was headed out the door barefooted. Willie and his family were just as poverty-stricken, but Willie stopped Jim in the front yard and asked, "Jim, don't you have no shoes?" Jim replied, "No, sir."
>
> Without hesitation, Willie slid off his own shoes and gave them to Jim to make the trip. Jim gratefully pulled on the slightly oversized shoes and walked over to the girl's house, ate popcorn, and had a lot of fun. I never will forget this, later in life, Willie was married with three kids, fell ill, and was having a hard time financially. He phoned Uncle Jim and said, "Jim, I need to borrow twenty-five dollars for a water heater;

Swimming in the river: Mary Conroy Hobbs, John Petty Hobbs, and Nellie Conroy

ours just went out. I'll pay you the first of the month." Jim replied, "It's okay, Uncle, I'll be over in a minute." Jim drove over to Willie's house and promptly gave him fifty dollars. "Uncle Willie, don't you ever worry about paying me back; I've never forgotten those shoes you gave me that winter day. If there's anything you ever need, you call me."

While working on the various farms at the age of thirteen, John Petty was introduced to drinking. Every farmer going out to work in the field would carry a bottle of whiskey or moonshine in their pockets. On break, they would customarily pass the bottle around, never skipping the boy. Unfortunately, these little sips here and there brought on alcoholism, which would later mar his life and marriage.

Despite drinking heavily, John Petty would do anything for anyone, and he wasn't mean to a soul. He was a loving and humble father who spent quality time with his children, often taking them swimming, fishing, or out for Sunday drives to the country. He worked as a mechanic and always seemed to have a job, although he never had enough money to make ends meet. He met a lot of people and throughout his life helped a lot of people, but they didn't pay anything for his efforts. He always had a rough go of it as a result. Of course, back in those days, twenty-five to thirty dollars a week was average pay; every cent was pinched when you had six children and a wife to look after. On several occasions, Mary would rush ahead of her husband to pick up his paycheck to safeguard it from being consumed from inside a bottle.

John Petty married John A.'s mother for the first time on June 28, 1923, when he was just twenty-one years of age. Overall, they were happy together, although they experienced the usual ups and downs of marriage. Alcohol abuse would eventually take its toll on the relationship, leading to their first divorce. Both remarried, but after each of their second spouses passed away, they married each other again on April 11, 1977. Their children advised them not to go through with it because they couldn't get along the first time. Sure enough, they divorced for the second and last time. John Petty died in March of 1980 and Mary lived to be in her nineties, passing away in 1997. Although John A. never met his father's relatives or his maternal grandfather Valentine, he would carry with him their heritage for the rest of his life.

CHAPTER FOUR

Born for a Storm

John A. was born for a storm, no doubt, because everywhere he went was a big storm, and he had to plow his way through it.
—RONNIE HOBBS

There was no storm to be weathered on February 11, 1928, in West Nashville. The mean temperature was a cool but stable forty-five degrees Fahrenheit.[9] The high point of the day was the birth of a boy inside a quaint house at 1412 Natchez Trace, tucked between the H. G. Hill and Roger's grocery stores. Gasping for his first breath, this baby boy was destined for nothing short of a life of impact. In fact, John Anthony Hobbs was fated to be productive, as well as a quick learner with a mind filled with innovation and ideas.

Throughout his life, he would shrug off complacency and conventional ways, and strive to learn from his mistakes. An Aquarius is blessed with a gregarious and supportive personality, and excellent storytelling skills; throughout their lives, they magnetically draw people to them. These would be the many friends to whom John A. would attach great importance and surround

John Petty Hobbs holding his first son, John A., circa 1929.

himself with until one or the other's final breath was exhaled. Being born the first of six children forced this son into an early leadership role and most certainly helped mold him into a high achiever with maturity, self-discipline, and a desire to help and protect others.[10]

At the time of John A.'s birth, the world around the Hobbs family was far from tranquil. Prohibition was in full swing, and the Roaring Twenties would soon fade into the Great Depression. Beginning in August 1929, this epic period of economic hardship would last forty-three months. The full effects of the declining economy, however, weren't felt in Nashville until the Wall Street crash in October of that year. Most Tennesseans lost their jobs, and struggling farmers turned to their homemade stills to sell corn whiskey.[11] John's parents were not immune from the tough times, but they managed to start and raise a family in the midst of it all.

John A. was the oldest of six children—three boys and three girls. Next in age was his brother Kenneth (Ken) born in 1933, followed by Paul (1935), JoAnn (1939), Margaret (1943), and Patricia (Pat), born in 1946. As a kid, much of John A.'s life was really difficult for him. His mother had a hard time working long hours and raising six kids. Out of pure necessity, she called on her oldest son to assist with chores and look after his siblings. Under the stress and demands of

Kenneth Hobbs with big brother John A., circa 1935.

the family hardships, he morphed almost overnight into the role of a responsible adult. It was essential to Mary that her children were raised well. That's why she worked tirelessly to teach them values and a work ethic, and to instill in them the qualities necessary to succeed in a toilsome life.

> My mother helped me a lot when I was growing up. She taught me manners, so I knew how to act in public and not make a fool out of myself. You learned to just shut up, stand over to one side, listen, and learn. If you go out there and start talking too much, you get your ass in trouble, and you don't even know what you're talking about. I learned early

John A. playing cowboy, circa 1930.

on not to go on about what I can do and then find out I
couldn't do it.

Comforts such as running hot water and indoor plumbing
didn't exist at the Hobbses residence. Resourcefully, Mary boiled
water for washing in a black kettle out in the backyard. During
the winter months, she bathed each of her kids in a number-three
washtub; in summertime, the entire family would drive down
to the river to go swimming. This natural bath created one less
chore for Mom, and everyone thoroughly enjoyed themselves.

The family raised chickens, and Mary cooked eggs every way
imaginable on an old stove that used coal oil, with one burner.
You could turn the burner up and light it and then cook whatever
you had on it. It had an oven with two burners under it, and she
especially loved to bake biscuits in it.

The family had a rudimentary outside toilet, but the Work
Projects Administration (WPA) upgraded it to a "two-hole," when
they came through the area in 1938. The WPA was an agency
created as part of the New Deal to alleviate the effects of the Great
Depression in the area.[12]

> That meant we were "up-town" when we had two toilet
> seats! One hole for the adults and one for the children. They
> built the nicest outside toilet for twenty-five dollars.

The Hobbs family was stone broke, but so was everybody else
living around them. They didn't see things as rich or poor; they
thought everybody was the same. Most people didn't own a car,
but thanks to having a father who worked as a mechanic, the family
always managed to have at least one vehicle to share. Doors were
left unlocked primarily because there was nothing worth stealing.
The stifling summer heat and humidity were combated with the

use of one old, dilapidated box fan. No one had air conditioning in their homes, so kids simply opened the windows and dragged their beds in front of the screen door. They propped open the door at night and let the air blow through, leaving them sweating in the summer and freezing in the winter.

> In the wintertime, we kept warm with our monkey heater, a little bitty heater stove. We'd get that thing real hot at night, then stand by it in our long underwear. Once we were good and hot, we'd go jump in that bed really quick and it stayed pretty warm all night. I remember Dad telling us about waking up one time and snow had blown in through the roof and landed on his bed.

John A. attended Cathedral Catholic School through the first grade, where he was routinely picked up after school by his Aunt Nellie. One afternoon she was running late and John A. waited out front on the small concrete wall for her, not moving an inch. This turned out to be a big, messy mistake.

> I can remember when my daddy had an A-Model Ford, blue with a yellow stripe on it, and it was a hot car. My aunt had an A-Model Ford that was brown with a brown stripe on it. School let out and my aunt didn't meet me; she was running late. I sat down on a little concrete wall that's still there today and soon I needed to use the bathroom. I didn't know where to go, but I didn't want to go back inside the school. So, I sat there and messed in my short pants. When my aunt finally pulled up, she opened the car door and said, "Come on!" At first, I wouldn't get up. Finally, when I did get up, doo-doo just ran down my leg and, oh, she got mad. "Why didn't you go to the bathroom?" She ate me out, but I was so scared and didn't know what to do. She made me stand up on that

A-Model Ford, you know it had a little thing to hold on to,
until we got back up there where we lived. She wiped me off
with Kleenex and it was still running down my legs, so they
threw me in the bathtub and cleaned me up.

The following year John Petty and Mary bought and moved into
a small house at 19 Twin Street in West Nashville. John switched
schools and attended second grade at Saint Ann's Catholic School.
It was at Saint Ann's that John A. met and ran with a bunch of
kids who would become lifelong pals. Pat Mitchell, King Foxall,
and Robert Wolf were the best of friends. The hilarious stories
they would co-create would leave anyone wondering how in the
world they didn't get thrown out of school. Despite the harmless
shenanigans of school boys, and repeating the fourth grade, John
A. managed to graduate from Saint Ann's with an eighth grade
education. He not only gained solid friendships, but also the
influence and respect of a favorite teacher, Sister Mary Coleman,
whom he would one day repay with magnificent philanthropy.

At Saint Ann's I had a wonderful fourth-grade teacher, Sister
Mary Coleman. She liked me so well, she kept me for two
years in a row! I think I was raised at a good time in America.
We never had it that bad, but we had it bad enough. I think it
was a good time in my life. I made it good and I enjoyed life.

As a kid, John A. rode a bicycle everywhere he went. His
favorite destination was his grandmother's, because he always
had a nice time with her. She lived back at 1404 Natchez Trace,
just around the corner from the house in which he was born.
She wasn't affluent, but she had a nice big home that she lived
for years. Her neighbors were decent people who lived well and
treated John A. kindly. It was here, on his grandmother's side

of town, that he learned to mix with different classes of people, and he could talk and interact with anyone, regardless of their socioeconomic level.

Like most boys his age, John A. always found something entertaining to do. He especially loved playing sandlot ball with all the neighborhood kids on a small, vacant lot; every neighborhood seemed to have one. Two-Eye Catch, a game in which you batted and ran to a single base, was a favorite because the lot wasn't big enough to play much baseball. They used an old bat they had found somewhere and a ball taped over with electric tape covered with dirt to keep the tape in place. Other popular activities included swimming in the river, crossing the river at Clees' Ferry to reach his uncle's farm to ride Charlie Horse, or greeting the circus when it came to town. Without money for a circus show ticket, John A. had to be resourceful, never shying away from an opportunity to work.

> I used to go down when the circus came to town. On Friday, they would let us off school to go to Centennial Park, where they set everything up. We'd go down there on that Wednesday for the parade and see elephants walking and lions in a cage. Gargantuan was a big gorilla and they made a big deal out of marrying him with a female gorilla. We'd watch as they raised the tent poles with the mighty elephants, which were hooked to those large booms. We all went for the two o'clock show, and I'd pick up Coca-Cola bottles all around the grounds. There was a bench with a seat and another one to put your feet on that was hollow. If you were down under there picking up bottles, the girls sitting above would let their dresses fall down. If they stood up, you could see up their dresses. So, we would go down there and pick up the bottles and put them in a case to bring out. We

exchanged the bottles for a free pass to the night show, and there would be at least ten of us. We always had a big time and rode our bicycles home at midnight.

John A.'s early years were characterized by innocent fun with friends, riding bikes, swimming, flirting, carnivals, and games. However, as John A. aged, and children were added to the Hobbs family, responsibilities and expectations changed. His parents were struggling more than ever with only one income. Mary was forced to quit her telephone company job in order to be a homemaker and mother of six. This put a financial strain on the family that would force young John A. to work multiple jobs before and after school.

CHAPTER FIVE

A Childhood Skipped

*You know, I was a great believer when
I was coming up that you help everybody.*
—JOHN A. HOBBS

John A.'s mother leaned on him for help more than she did any of the other children. His father expected him to work as soon as he could get out of school, and John A. took on several jobs by the time he was twelve years old. He seemingly skipped childhood altogether, working for the newspaper, delivering groceries and telegrams, driving trucks, and contributing however else he could.

My parents could use the money, and I never thought of it as an obligation. I thought it was good that I could give the money to them. Back in those days I only made twenty-five dollars a week when I worked for the newspaper, and I gave them most of it. Everybody worked, and if you could get a job, you went to work. Even when you were twelve or thirteen years old, you were out doing something. I never had a teenage life; I went to work when I was young. I never went

> to a prom, football game, or played any team sports. The
> only baseball I got to play was in an empty lot with an old
> ball that we taped up. I knew what hard times were.

John A. worked for the paper in the press room and composing room and as a delivery boy, a common position available to boys in the 1940s, and he had a lot of fun working at it. School started every morning at 7:30 AM, so the paper route began earlier, at 4:30 AM, at which time he started rolling up the papers and preparing them for delivery. This was the perfect opportunity to read the sports page about the Joe Louis fight or to stay current on world news. The newspaper man they worked for was kind and willing to assist with difficult or distant deliveries by driving the heaviest loads of papers out and dropping them off at a closer destination.

To deliver papers on his bicycle, John A. would tie the conveniently stacked and bundled papers onto the front and back luggage rack of his bike, which fit perfectly and was balanced for riding. Riding a bicycle was the most popular form of transportation for teens, and in the 1940s one might ride a popular brand such as a Western Flyer or Montgomery Ward's Elgin, but the best one was generally considered to be the New Departure. There was a Schwinn bicycle as well, but few people could afford it.

John rode the hell out of his Western Flyer bicycle, which he bought new for fifteen dollars. These bikes were gearless, so you really had to pedal them hard to keep them going. There were two types of hubs, and John A.'s bicycle had a bar hub about two and a half inches across. One of the first skills John A. learned was to take the hub off every two or three months and wash it in gasoline. He had to learn to grease the bike, front and back, and then adjust everything so that the wheels wouldn't rub a fender, causing friction. Having a father as a mechanic meant that the necessary supplies and grease were conveniently kept on hand in the shop. In fact, with his father's help, John became so proficient at bicycle repair and maintenance that the eighth grade school newspaper advertised his very first business in it, "Hobbses Bicycle Shop."

> I packed it with new grease, then put it back together and washed it off. I washed it in gas to get all that old oil out of it and to get it down to the raw metal. This process made it look brand-new. You could run your hand up in there where you had a lot of washers in it and those were your brakes. I was the only kid in school that could tear them apart and put them back together, and I could ride the hell out of a bicycle back then.

When you're riding a gearless bike in Nashville, you quickly learn where the hills are. You could make it up a long grade, such as three-mile-long Charlotte Pike all right, but you definitely tried to avoid the steep hills. John A. found a method that worked even better than dodging hills, called "hanging trucks."

> Fertilizer trucks used to come and go from the local West Nashville plant all the time. We'd hang those trucks, you know, grab the side of them and let them tow us into town. Nowadays, they would shoot you for it, but back then, we did it all the time. We used to sit on a curb and wait for the trucks to come by every ten or fifteen minutes. When they stopped at Fifty-First Avenue, they would chug starting back up. Soon they would get around the corner and we would just grab onto it and the truck would get up to fifty or sixty miles an hour. We would just hold on with one hand and if they got going too fast, we'd say, "Ah hell, we better

turn loose." We hanged many a truck in our day to avoid riding those steep hills.

The boys carried their papers along Charlotte Pike and Fifty-First Avenue, and through an area called the Nations. This part of town was so-named because of all the mixed nationalities of whites who lived there. Every street had the name of a different state, and the Nations was considered to be a rough part of town. If any that did not belong dared to cross the creek boundary into this area, they were immediately "rocked back" to their side of town.

> I knew most of them on both sides of the creek, and they never bothered the paper boy. People were good to me, and I was good to them in return. I didn't try to steal from them or do anything bad, so they left me alone.

By far, the most interesting destination for delivering the newspaper was the nearby penitentiary. The Tennessee State Penitentiary looms over the Nations neighborhood in West Nashville with an omnipotent architecture. It was built in 1895 to house eight hundred inmates, and at its busiest was bulging with more than four thousand prisoners. The penitentiary also housed the state's electric chair, which was used in the execution of 125 death row inmates. Since being closed in 1992, it has been the site of several movies, including *The Green Mile*, starring Tom Hanks.[13] Today, the penitentiary is off-limits to the public, in widespread disrepair, and emanates eerie vibes. John recalls his experiences delivering the paper out there in the early forties.

> When I was a kid, I worked everywhere. I even delivered papers every morning to the State Penitentiary, which had a metal detector in the lobby you had to go through. This was

way back in the early forties. They had a sign in there that read, "Inmates Today: 453." We'd get there sometime in the morning, close to six, and when they electrocuted somebody out there, the lights really went dim. The street lights outside of the prison went dim and then it would brighten up, get dim again, then brighten up. They needed the majority of power for "Old Sparky" and they would electrocute first thing in the morning before everybody was awake and the lights wouldn't be burning. I used to go over to death row and carry my papers in there, which was out in the middle of the pen. It had the electrocution chair out there and it had maybe twelve or fifteen cells. Each one of them had a private cell because they would hang themselves or kill somebody. I was never scared when I carried thirty-five to forty papers down there. Some didn't want or care about the news, but many would buy it. The trustee used to walk me through, and he was in there for killing his wife. I used to kid him a lot, I was just a little old kid, I wasn't maybe twelve years old.

I'd say, "Did you really kill your wife?"

He'd say, "Ah, no. Hell, I was framed, I am innocent."

All the inmates were "innocent." They never would admit to anything, but he'd laugh and cut up with me. Back then, they paid the prisoners a silver dollar a day for labor. They made license plates for the cars, they had gardens and a big, four-hundred-acre farm. There was a lower farm, and the men worked the fields and grew vegetables, and the women inmates worked the cannery. They canned stuff for the blind school, the insane asylum, and the TIS Boys School. They really took care of a lot of things out at the old pen and they all worked. They paid for the newspaper in silver dollars. I'd take a little bag every Saturday down to the bank, not knowing what they'd be worth today, but back then they were only worth a dollar. Silver dollars are pretty heavy when you are carrying fifty of them.

Young John A. carried the paper route morning and night. On Saturdays, he found a job delivering groceries out of the back of an old 1940 Chevrolet. At just twelve years old, he acquired his driver's license and made three dollars a day, which he thought was good money. In those days, if you made a hundred twenty dollars per week, you were considered a high-paid employee.

I went and got my license when I was real young because when I was driving a hay truck, the old man said, "You've got to have a license to drive that truck!" So, I went and obtained a driver's license, but I lied and told them I was sixteen when I wasn't. My age was so screwed up, I had the wrong car license, I had the wrong age everywhere. I

John A.'s drivers' license photo, circa 1940.

went to work on a farm cutting and hauling hay. The owner had a large flatbed truck with four or five gears on it, and he didn't have anyone to drive it, so Dad came and got me.

"Will you drive a hay truck? Come on, I am going to put you in it!"

I said, "Dad, I can't change that many gears; I've only used a three-shift gear going from first and second to high. That truck has five or six gears in it!"

"You can do it, let's go!"

We went out to the farm and I just kept the hay truck in high gear and drove slowly. We had two men up on the back of the truck, and they would stack the hay up as we went. As soon as the truck was loaded with hay, Dad would get in and drive the truck to the barn and let them unload it. Then I'd drive it back to the field empty. They wouldn't let me drive with a full load on it because they were afraid I would turn it over.

In addition to the newspaper route, grocery delivery, and driving hay trucks, John delivered telegrams. It was his most emotionally challenging job. One day he delivered some tragic news to an elderly woman, forever changing both of their lives.

I rode all the way out from West Nashville to downtown to take a telegram, which had to be delivered to an address in a neighborhood I just rode from. I never will forget, she was up in her late sixties and had a little apron rolled up like my grandmother. She had her hair pulled up in a bow and the apron went around her neck and then rolled up. It was summertime, and I parked my bike in the yard, walked up, and knocked on her door. She had the door open, but the screen was fastened. The elderly woman came to the door and said, "Yes?"

I said, "I've got a telegram for Mrs. So-and-so," and she said, "That's me."

She seemed like such a nice lady and reminded me of my grandmother. She was cooking supper, and I remember asking her if she had anything burning inside? She said, "No, I set it off the stove when I heard you knock." She had an old coal stove, and she was cooking with that.

She unlatched the door and snatched the telegram from my hand before signing for it. I had to have a signed receipt for the office as proof I delivered the message. As soon as she took the telegram, she opened it up and read it. It said, "We deeply regret to inform you that your son has been killed in action in the European Theater." She almost went to the floor, and I was just a little kid. I wasn't over thirteen, and

I grabbed her and said, "Are you by yourself?"

She said, "Yes, but my other son will be home in about thirty minutes."

I said, "Well, come over to the porch swing here."

I walked her over to the swing, and she put her head on my shoulder and she sobbed. I thought, "Oh, my God," and I felt so sorry.

She said, "He was a good boy. Maybe it's a mistake?"

I said, "Let's hope it is. I hope they find him and every-thing works out for you."

I gently pulled out the slip and asked, "Do you mind signing this for me?" She signed it, and I stood up to go, but I just couldn't leave her there by herself, so I sat back down next to her for another thirty minutes. I thought, "Well, I have to ride a bicycle all the way back downtown and back again", and I told her I had to get back. "Do you want me to help you inside or anything?"

She said, "My son ought to be here any minute."

I told her that I sincerely wished I could help her, walked out to where I had left my bicycle, and rode off. I told them when I returned to the office, "Don't give me any more tele-grams like that! I refuse to carry them." It touched me, and I have thought about her many times since. I even went back one day to see her, but I never went in. I don't know what I would have said to her. The house sat vacant for many years and just recently was bulldozed to make room for new housing units.

John A. was a good soul with a big heart and wanted to help in every way he could, and this was often taken for granted. His loved ones leaned on him hard for so much at such a young age and applied constant pressure on their eldest son to help his family. Although he learned how to do many different things when he was young, it all came at a high price. There was no teenage life for him. Overnight, he went from being a kid to a young adult taking on other mature responsibilities, such as being the designated driver whenever his father drank too much. Unfortunately, this all too often was the case.

The war had already started, and they were building camp forests. I couldn't have been over thirteen years old when I went with my dad one night to Tullahoma, where he worked on heavy equipment. I knew all the men, including a guy named Dick Smith, who ran the bulldozer. They shot craps, drank, and worked on trucks. They had a brand-new '42 dump truck with tandem wheels on it and, boy, that thing had the gears in it. It was after midnight, and Dad got drunker than hell and couldn't drive us home.

Dick asked, "Can you drive that truck?"

"I've never driven anything that big!"

He said, "Look, you got Dad in the truck and he's tapped out. I am going to put it in the right gear, show you, then I am going to jump off the truck, but don't you stop!"

He got up there and had the door open, and he's telling me how to do it. I get it rolling forward in the right gear and then he jumps off. Now, we're in Tullahoma, that's about eighty miles out of Nashville. I am driving the speed limit, back then about thirty-five miles an hour. I get down to Nashville, and I'd say it's about two-thirty in the morning so there's no traffic on the road. I would time it and watch the red lights where I wouldn't have to change gears. Dad was sound asleep, I mean he was out. I get to Broad Street, then to Second Avenue.

I am driving that truck and making it jump, clutching it. I'd give it a lot of gas and clutch it and make it bump, but then I hit that first red light. Lights were timed where they would change only at certain times, and I'd go slower so I didn't have to stop. I believe I'd run the red light even if it turned, because I didn't think anybody was out on the road. I drove on out to Murphy Road and went on through. Got to Charlotte at Forty-Sixth. I thought, "Damn, that red light's going to get me!" I am clutching it and I get it through there and finally made the turn. I drove it home and pulled up in our front yard. We had an old gravel driveway there, and I pulled up and turned it off. "Whew!" I thanked God that we got home. I couldn't wake Dad up, so I went on in the house and Momma says, "Where's your dad?"

"He's out in the truck."

"Is he drunk?"

I replied, "Well, yeah."

She came out in her housecoat, and we finally got Dad out of the truck.

"Did you drive that truck from Tullahoma?"

"Yeah, Dick Smith got me started and I drove it on in."

"My God!"

We managed to get Dad in bed and the next morning when he got up, he was drinking coffee and said with a smile, "You must have made it pretty good, didn't ya?"

Many times, when work was finished, the Hobbs family gathered to listen to their Western Auto radio they kept in a large cabinet. There were sports to listen to such as the Joe Louis fights or baseball games, news with the *Fireside Chats* and soap operas like *Young Widow Brown*, *Lorenzo Jones*, and *Ma Perkins*. At night, there was Edward G. Robinson in *Mr. DA*, Jack Benny, and Irish singer Dennis Day. On Saturday nights, John A. came home and his dad had the radio blasting out the Grand Ole Opry.

> I had a good life and although West Nashville was a poor
> neighborhood, we didn't have to lock our doors. There was
> no killing, no stabbing, or anything of that nature. I always
> kidded everyone that it was the poorest neighborhood in
> Nashville. Everybody had three cars. Two jacked up and one
> running.

Serious crime might not have been present around the Hobbs family, but they felt the effects of prejudice for being Catholics. Living in the Bible Belt, many of the families didn't want their children hanging with John A. because of his faith, calling their kids back into the house immediately if they eyed them playing together.

> The parents would get me aside and ask, "Do you really think
> you can go in a box and tell your sins and go to heaven?"
> I would answer, "Well, I was taught that as an altar boy,
> and that's all I know."
> They would question me about the church and thought
> I was weird because we were Catholics. We thought the Church
> of Christ followers were weird because they didn't believe
> in music, and they didn't think that anyone but themselves
> could get to heaven. Momma told me once if I ever went
> into a Church of Christ, she would beat me to death. Damn!
> Later I dated a Church of Christ girl, went inside her church,
> and everybody told Momma! A lot of the families would call
> their kids in the house. They'd say, "Jesse, come on in here.
> Don't you be out there with that Catholic." They thought I
> was a weirdo or something.

John A. learned to steer clear of serious trouble and used his unshakeable moral compass on more than one occasion to keep on the right side of the law. He never ran with anyone that got into serious trouble, mainly because his mother had been really good at raising him. She taught him good from bad, and he gives her a lot of credit for the lessons that led him down the straight path.

> We could have all went to the pen out there, but the crowd I ran with, we never did anything serious to get in that kind of trouble. I often thought how close it was; we could have gone either way because a lot of people we played with went to the penitentiary out of West Nashville.
>
> I'll tell you what happened one night. We were out in Richland Park, and they closed at eleven o'clock, but we'd stay up there after the park was closed. All of us boys would be up there and sometimes there would be a few girls. Across the street from the park, there were all these little stores. Well, King Foxall and my good friend Pat Mitchell were with me, but two other old boys were hanging out in the park at the same time as us. They were bad news and had already been in the service and home now having been dishonorably discharged. They called over to us and said, "Hey, let's rob that store over there. Come on!"
>
> Pat, King, and I were scared of these guys, so we all went over across the street, but stayed behind them. As those hoodlums went around back to break into the store, Pat, King, and I took off running as fast as we could for home, about a mile and a half, but we got our asses out of there quick. The police caught those two old boys later that night, and they went to the pen over it. Thank God, my friends and I had already run back home and gone to bed by the time that all happened.

There was a very wealthy and well-known bootlegger in West Nashville named Cecil Collins. John A. ran with his son and daughter, and Cecil used to pass by driving an expensive new

Cadillac convertible. Everyone around there knew that he owned a liquor store, so John A. swore that when he was grown, he, too, was going to buy a liquor store. By the time he was done, John A. and his family bought three liquor stores!

Mr. Jones was another notorious resident of West Nashville who John A. knew and liked. He was a nice enough fella, but he just couldn't help but steal. He was much older than John A., and he once told him, "I can't help but steal, it's in my blood! I don't even need it and I steal. I don't know what the hell is wrong with me?"

He got out of the pen in '46 and he went into hauling whiskey, still as wild as ever. One night, he cut a hole in the roof of a local jewelry store and swiped all the watches and diamonds. He had a '48 Mercury that he took the hubcaps off and placed all the stolen jewelry inside. The police knew he was the one that committed the crime, but they didn't have enough proof to send him back to the pen. The police pulled him over the next day on Harding Place and searched his car, not thinking to check inside the hubcaps. Of course, they found nothing and Mr. Jones was free to go. As he pulled away, the police heard the *ding, clank, ding* noises the stolen jewelry made inside the wheels. The police immediately pulled him over again, and this time they searched inside the hubcaps. Finding the stolen goods, they sentenced him to either a life in prison or to leave the state of Tennessee and never return. Of course, Mr. Jones chose the travel option and went off to California. He stayed there for most of his life before returning to Tennessee as an elderly man.

John A. was aware that if he stayed in West Nashville, there was a good chance that he would end up in the pen with a lot of the people he knew and grew up with. He was raised well and had solid integrity thanks to his family and early work experiences. It didn't take long for him to see that if he wanted a better life for himself and for those he loved, he would have to leave the poverty and bad influences of West Nashville far behind.

CHAPTER SIX

Merchant Marine

There is no security on this earth; there is only opportunity.
—DOUGLAS MACARTHUR

John A. entered World War II when he was just fifteen years old, an age when most young men are going into ninth grade. There was no security in John A.'s home life, and he was about to thrust himself into a tumultuous world filled with constant change and limitless opportunities. This was a global war that lasted from 1939 until 1945 involving many of the world's nations. It included all the great powers eventually forming two opposing military alliances, the Allies and the Axis. The Allies, led by the United States, Soviet Union, United Kingdom, and China, worked to stop the aggression of the Axis powers—Germany, Italy, and Japan. It was the most widespread war in history and directly involved more than one hundred million people. There were millions of fatalities, making it the deadliest conflict in human history. During this time, Japan was focused on dominating the Pacific and Asia. However, with its critical loss in the Battle of Midway, Japan and the Axis advance was halted in 1942. With the capture of key Western Pacific Islands, the Allies all but crippled the Japanese navy. The Japanese refused to surrender under the Allies' terms, which forced the United States to drop two catastrophic atomic bombs in August 1945. One was dropped on Hiroshima and the other on Nagasaki, ending the war in Asia and securing total victory for the Allies in World War II.[14]

Let's backtrack a couple of years, going back to when John A. was fifteen. He finished the eighth grade in 1943 and realized that his family needed more assistance than he could manage with the odd jobs around town. Hearing the news that you could enlist in Birmingham, Alabama, he and his childhood friend, King Foxall, quit delivering newspapers and caught an early morning Greyhound bus for a dollar and a half, bound for Alabama.

> My family was having an awful hard time. Dad was drinking pretty heavily and it got worse. He kept a job until he got up in his sixties and then he got to where he wasn't working. I went down there and enlisted and left, but I sent most of my allotment check home to my family. I sent them all I could, which was two-thirds of what I made.

Arriving in early June at the Empire Building, where all the recruiting offices were located, John A. and King naively thought they could simply sign up and go off to war right away. With the necessary paperwork filled out, the two boys headed upstairs for their physicals. King had a bad arm that wouldn't straighten out, and they turned him down for service almost immediately. John A. passed the first part of the physical with flying colors and headed upstairs for the final requirement, a dental exam. He was finally stamped "approved" at close to four o'clock in the afternoon, only to find out from the recruiters the offices closed in thirty minutes. They were disheartened by the news which meant that they would have to come back the next day so John A. could finish the process.

Unprepared for an overnight in Birmingham, they put together what little coinage they had and shared one hamburger for supper. A hotel was out of the question, so they bedded down among the homeless in the park across the street from the Empire Building. Watching the survival techniques of the local homeless men, they pulled two double benches together and gathered up used newspaper to shield themselves from the dew that would render them cold and wet all night. The teens carefully watched as the homeless man next to them dug out additional papers from the trash in the middle of the night, replacing the ones that were already wet. John A. and King followed suit, changing papers about three times that night. Despite their efforts, they awoke in the park the next morning, drenched. Not only was John A. too young at the time to join the service, he didn't have his parent's permission either. Thinking on his feet, John A. paid fifty cents to a homeless man to forge his mother's signature. With King waiting out front, John A. signed up with the Merchant Marines and received orders to leave for boot camp in Florida in two weeks. Riding the bus back home, he knew that upon his return, he had no choice but to tell his mother what he had done.

Two weeks later, John A. returned alone to begin his basic training. Scared and not knowing exactly what to expect, John A. was transported by train through Birmingham, Alabama, to Saint Petersburg, Florida, for boot camp.

> They would stop to load and unload while keeping us in the car, so we all got to know each other. One old boy was "Fats" from a little old town outside of Petersburg, Florida. We nicknamed him "Fats" and they all called me "Sleepy Hobbs"

because of my dreamy eyes. I'd never seen the ocean and had my first sight of it that week. I just couldn't believe it. We got to boot camp and all I could think was, "What have I done?"

We arrived late in the evening and they gave us uniforms and fatigues to wear and shaved our heads. They were good barracks with two beds together and maybe a hundred-people sleeping in one big room. All of them were in their underwear and T-shirts, and for the first time in my life, I heard grown men cry. I was lying in bed and you could hear them *sob, sniffle,* and *whimper.* One old, big, and tough boy jumped up and hit the floor in the middle of the night. He said, "The next one that cries, I am going to knock the hell out of them myself! Now, go to bed!" I covered my head up and stayed in bed, but boy he was mad. He wanted to go to sleep and didn't give a damn where he was at. I thought to myself, "I am not going to say anything," but I never cried. I never even thought about crying, but I was stunned at some big, tough-looking guys that cried like a baby the first time they were away from home. The next night, we got to cutting up in the barrack, and they made us put our backpacks on and march up and down the pier for two hours in the middle of the night. Boy, we didn't do that anymore, when they cut them lights out, we went to bed!

John A. was relieved when they placed him on a water tender boat instead of the sailing ship because he didn't want to climb the large masts. The water tender hauled equipment, soldiers, and supplies to the war front for the Allies, and upon return the ship had to take on water in the hulls to stabilize it and prevent it from flipping over in storms. Most of the ships had four hulls. Two in the bow and two in the stern. The men would sleep in the middle section. When they reloaded the ship, they simply pumped the water out.

The men endured some grueling exercises in Key West, Florida including rowing in the heat of the day until they had blisters on their hands.

> They had us rowing, and I asked the chief, "If the ship sinks, do we have to row this thing to land?" He laughed and said, "Just row until you get tired."

They had water coolers on the main ship, but they wouldn't turn them on. They believed drinking cold water in extreme heat was unhealthy for you, so they insisted on drinking only luke-warm water, which tasted salty and not at all thirst quenching. There were many lessons before shipping out, but there was one more challenging exercise that would forever be etched in John A.'s mind, jumping off the boat. John A. recounts the training exercise which tested his fear of jumping from extreme heights.

> The training staff would swing a large boom, like a crane, out from the ship for us to jump off into the water about seventy feet below. You hold onto your life jacket and jump. I never had jumped from that height and the first day we went off that thing, I thought I never would resurface. When you hit the water from that high, you're holding onto your life jacket because it could break your neck if you didn't. We popped up out of that water because the life jackets were the old cork kind and they just shoot you right out of the water. So, I jumped and shot out of the water and said, "Whew God, I hope I don't do that anymore."
>
> The next day we were back doing the same exercise, but this time I made the mistake of looking down. The guy in front of me refused to jump and they threatened to kick

> him out of the service. When it came time for me to jump I said, "I can't jump!" The trainer yelled at me to get off that boom, but it was no use. There were at least three of us that couldn't muster the courage to jump the second time around, and they never kicked us out of the service.

Unfortunately, the rigors of boot camp were just the beginning for young John A. He thought often about just telling his superiors his real age and going back home. He was there because he needed the money, and although he hated boot camp at first, he actually began to enjoy the adventure of it. The experience was something new for him, and he learned a tremendous amount in a very short time. He especially learned how to respect authority and other people from all backgrounds. With basic training behind him, he shipped out on an army transport service ship, the *SS Cuba*. With so many troops on board, he inevitably ran into some interesting characters.

> They took two older men that had been to the penitentiary, and they were probably in their early forties. We slept in a great big room with bunks on each side, stacked two high. They put these two in there with us and they told us they just got out of the pen on agreement to sign on. We were in New Orleans, shipping out the next day, and I came back aboard ship that night about midnight. Those two men were harassing this boy, and he was playing like he was drunk and tapped out because he was so scared. I walked on over to where he was and they were putting matches between his toes and lighting them to give him a "hot foot."
>
> I yelled, "Hey, fellas, don't do that!", and I yanked the matches out. I thought those two guys could have killed me, but I said, "That isn't any way to treat that boy. He can't take care of himself, so go on to bed and leave that boy alone!"

They said, "Ah, nah, we were just horsin' around." Luckily, they went on to bed and left him alone because they knew they couldn't afford to get in trouble and go back to the pen. Still it was wrong for them to do it.

I was just turning sixteen and this guy on the ship had his brother, Joe, there. Joe couldn't read or write, and his brother wanted me to look after him because he had never been out on the ship or anywhere for that matter. I thought, "Here he is two years older than me, he ought to be looking after me!" Really, I was a lucky man. I was on a ship running in Panama, South America, Puerto Rico, the Caribbean, and everywhere. In total, I made seven trips on five different ships before heading out to the Pacific Theatre.

John A.'s character and integrity did not go unnoticed on the *SS Cuba*, and he quickly turned down his first offer for promotion, following his heart and friends to the Pacific.

When I was on the *SS Cuba*, there was a man on there that was a second officer. He drank an awful lot and kept whiskey in his room, but he liked me and one night he said, "You know you're going to make a good man and a good sailor. We're going to be changing a lot of crew and some are shipping out to the Pacific. If you'll stay on, I'll move you up to chief petty officer. It's a big promotion for you; you'll be next to a noncommissioned officer."

"I know what I'd be," I replied, "but I don't really want to be a chief petty officer. Besides, the chief steward already asked me if my roommate Jay Barrilleaux and I would go to the Pacific on a new ship with him."

The chief steward was a good man and was over the entire cooking department. We were all good friends, so we signed up and packed our bags to go and pick up the new ship headed for the Pacific.

John A. had a short leave before departing on his new assignment and headed home to see his family, which he hadn't done for months. His mother had only one request before he shipped out again; to get a picture taken in his uniform and send it to her. John A. had this picture taken when he was seventeen years old at the station in New Orleans.

John A. in his dress uniform for Mom, circa 1945.

Mamma never took many pictures in our lifetime because back then cameras where hard to get. There was a box camera that Eastman Kodak made called the Brownie, but we couldn't afford one. My mother told me one day, when I was getting ready to go to church and wore a sport coat, she asked, "Would you do me one favor? Please get a picture of you in uniform. I'd just love to have a picture. Everybody's got a picture of their son in uniform and you never have taken one." So, I went down, when I was at the station in New Orleans, and they took one and they mailed it to her. She was so glad to get it.

"When you go to church next Sunday, will you wear your uniform?"

"Yes, I promise you, I'll wear it next Sunday."

I put it on that next Sunday and wore it up to church. Oh, she sat with me and told everybody, "This is my son and he's in the service." She was so proud of me and it embarrassed me, but it was nice of her to say that.

CHAPTER SEVEN

Ship Ahoy!

I wasn't no handsome star or anything like that.
You know, I made sense. I was ahead of my years.
—JOHN A. HOBBS

John A. and his friends were soon headed to the Pacific Theater to island hop, while repairing and replacing aircraft components on a class of cargo ship called a liberty ship. The *SS Nathanial Scudder*, named after a Revolutionary War hero, was 441 feet long, constructed in Houston, Texas, and modified in Mobile, Alabama. This class of cargo ship was dubbed the "Ugly Duckling" by *Time* Magazine and considered a "dreadful looking thing" by President Franklin D. Roosevelt. On average, they were mass manufactured in forty-two days in eighteen different shipyards throughout the United States. It was believed that these ships would help bring "liberty" to Europe, so they earned the name "liberty ships."

Ship ahoy! April 1944, age sixteen.

Altogether, six liberty ships were converted into floating aircraft repair depots in 1944. The secret project, dubbed "Project Ivory Soap," provided mobile depot support for B-29 bombers and P-51 Mustang fighters. These six ARU(F)'s—short for Aircraft Repair Unit, Floating—were also fitted with landing platforms to accommodate four Sikorsky R-4 helicopters, which were used to provide emergency medical evacuation of combat-injured personnel. In fact, these helicopters were the first helicopters to fly over Japan. Onboard the SS Nathanial Scudder were a mix of military branches with twenty-three officers and 362 enlisted men. An American air force lieutenant colonel commanded each ship; however, the ship's captain, engine room crew, and deck officers were Merchant Marines like John A. The navy provided the sailors to man the armament and to provide any remaining crew necessary.

To the men who served on the ship, it was their home away from home, their place of work, and it carried them safely across thousands of miles of ocean. While in the middle of the Pacific Ocean on May 5, 1945, the army sent orders to change the name of the ship from the SS Nathaniel Scudder to the SS Brigadier General Alfred J. Lyon.[15] When John A. first boarded the SS Nathanial Scudder, he only knew a few other men. With his outgoing and friendly, southern personality, however, he soon made lifelong friends with many of the crew, regardless of rank or age.

> You don't know everybody on the ship, but I knew a lot of them by sight. I'd pick a hundred men on the ship I probably knew and sometimes we'd go down and play cards at night, and we all had a good time together. We had a nice room with four lavatories, two commodes and two showers. So, it was really nice, much nicer than home. I was using the toilet in the backyard at my house, so I thought I was really

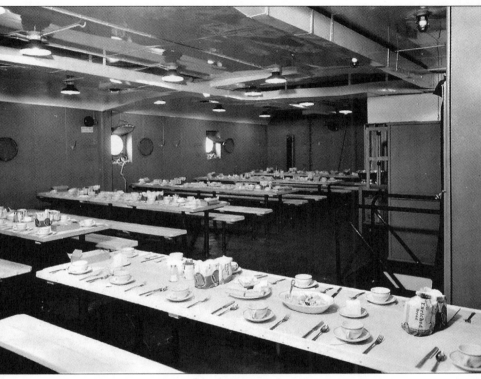

Mess hall in the SS Brig. Gen. Alfred J. Lyon.

uptown. We had a barbershop and a laundry, which wasn't always the case. Some of the ships I was on didn't have a laundry. You'd have to take your clothes and run a rope through your leg and tie the rope off and let it spin in the water and it would help clean them.

I was well liked and I could take care of myself. That was it: take care of yourself because there wasn't anybody there to look out for you. I learned about life, I learned about people, I learned about the ones that were different, too. When I went on the ship, all those guys were older than me, but they were all special people. The oldest guy was drafted in his forties. These were happy times in my life, and I enjoyed myself. I went on five different ships before I transferred to the ship I stayed on the longest. I learned more on my last ship because those guys were more settled. They weren't drunkards or wine heads; they were trained and skilled in many things. I learned a lot, and they were well-educated because most of them were college graduates. I knew all the officers from working in the mess hall, and they all became good friends of mine.

I was also a gunner's mate on a sixty-caliber gun. There were store rooms directly below the gun turret where the guns and ammunition were kept, and the shell was about six inches long. As gunner's mates, we had to put the guns on and the other guy would shoot them. If he was shot, sick or hurt, then one of us would have to take over the shooting. It wasn't anything bad because I couldn't hit the broad side of a barn if I tried. Working in the mess hall, we were waiters to the officers.

Well, this old colonel kind of liked us and one day he asked, "Y'all real busy?"

"No, sir."

"Well sit down here. I want to tell you about Borneo."

We grabbed a cup of coffee and sat with him and he told us like we were somebody we weren't. He started telling us about the fight in Borneo and how he volunteered our ship to go down there and assist. Fortunately, they didn't send us all the way to Borneo. Instead, they stopped us off at the next island up. I never will forget Joe from New Orleans got so mad. He complained, "That codger has led his life and now he's trying to get us all killed. I don't want to go to Borneo! I don't even know where the damn place is at!"

We had thirty-two officers on board. Some of them were the enlisted man's friend, humble and good, but many of them were a little cocky, hot shots. They chose people to be chief petty officers that were kind of smart-asses who thought they were really something. Hell, they didn't have but two stripes, whatever the hell that means. I never cared about the rating, I never cared about any of that. If I was the lowest man or the highest, I wouldn't have cared either way.

CHAPTER EIGHT

Banana Pie

There were things that we didn't understand.
Things that were way above us, but General MacArthur
thought he was the greatest thing on earth.
—JOHN A. HOBBS

When John A. shipped out, he never had eaten food that good in his life. Back home the family ate a lot of chicken because they raised them, and meat was a luxury they just couldn't afford. So John A.'s mother cooked a lot of eggs, every way imaginable, to feed her family, and many times, they ate eggs for breakfast, lunch, and supper.

I sent money to my mother, maybe fifty dollars a month, because there was nowhere to spend it on the ship. Coca-Colas and ice cream were free. Others complained about the food, but not me. I said, "Heck, that's the best damn food I'd ever eaten." The only thing I ever ate in my life was a hamburger and usually cereal or eggs for breakfast. The ship served hotcakes and foods that I never had heard of the names for. It was famous names like Hungarian goulash. I didn't know what Hungarian goulash was, so I ordered some. I had never seen Welsh rabbit on toast either. I thought it was real rabbit, but it's melted cheese with a little hot sauce poured over two pieces of toast.

We made our own bread on the ship, but you couldn't eat it for the first two days because the cooks said there was something unhealthy in the yeast. We had to wait until the bread was two days old before eating it. I went from 135 pounds to 165 on the ships because I had never eaten so well in my life. I just couldn't imagine what those guys must have eaten at home if they complained about food like this.

When we reached our first island in the Pacific, we saw bananas growing wild. I thought they grew down, but actually they grow upward. We went over to the island, and we all picked two or three stalks, put them in the lifeboat, and brought them back. Our chief cook, Shorty, from Texas, said, "I am gonna make y'all some banana pies!" He made us some banana cream pies, and it was the first fruit we ate on ship. Shorty hollered at me down the mess hall, "When you get off, come by the kitchen." I went by the kitchen, and he made me my own banana pie. "I want you to have this, take it to the room." He gave me a whole pie and I reached over and got me a spoon, and I ate that whole damn pie! I sat in my room down there and just ate. I hadn't had anything sweet and I thought, "Ooh, boy, this is the best pie."

We did leave with a lot of chocolate bars and different candies in the ship's post exchange, but when we opened the packages up, they were full of bugs! We were going to throw them over board, but one of the guys, smarter than the rest of us, exclaimed, "Don't do that!" He gathered all the bug-ridden candy and put it in a box, later trading it with locals for food, whiskey, screwing, and everything else. It was so smart of him and I learned something that day. That's the way you make money!

The men would go ashore at different places and they had a lot of fun, but by the time they arrived at the province of Tacloban in the Philippines after three months at sea, they were going stir crazy. The captain told half of the men they could go ashore to swim, provided they didn't leave the beach because there was shooting nearby in the mountains. John A. was glad to be in the bunch that was going over. As soon as they came ashore, he and a few mates went straight to town. It was a decision they would later regret.

We hit the province of Tacloban, where fighting was still going on in the mountains. The five of us were really just sick and tired of the sea and headed straight for town, where they sold Coca-Colas in the bottle like we had at home. They put moonshine whiskey in the bottle and put a cork down in it to keep it from spilling. It was rot-gut stuff, but we bought it and had a big time. I had never been that drunk; I might have been sixteen. I guess I drank a little in my life, but we got so drunk that we missed the boat back to the ship that night.

American soldiers placed us over to one side in the stockade with all these Japanese prisoners and a big spotlight shining down. The American soldiers had put us there, where we wouldn't wind up in the mountains because it was dangerous. The next morning, the soldiers laughed and said, "You better get out of there." We got up and went over to the dock, but couldn't get a boat back to the ship, anchored about three blocks away. We could see our ship firing up with the boilers running, smoke coming out, and it was fixing to leave us behind. We stole a bamboo, outrigger boat to row out to the ship, but when the first wave hit us, the damn bamboo boat turned over. Now drenched, we got the boat upright again and finally learned to get through that first wave. We rowed it out there to the ship, but the gangplank was pulled up, so we rowed beside it and hollered up. The captain came out on the bridge and ordered, "Lower the gangplank, and let those men board!" They lowered it down where we could jump off and kick the bamboo boat out and away.

"You men come up here, I want to talk to you!" We looked bad; we hadn't shaved and our clothes were soaked with salt water and now diluted vomit from our night before. He was the captain of the whole ship and he ate us out and looked pretty mad.

He said, "I want to ask you something. What would you have done if this ship had left?"

I answered, "Well, I'd have gone to the airport and tried to fly over with an army plane."

He said, "That's pretty good thinking, but you might not have made it, and we weren't coming back for you, that's for sure! Why in the hell did all of you go into town? You had no business going into town, and you could have been killed!"

I was the youngest on the ship and the old man with us was in his forties, which I considered old.

He said, "Well, we wanted to get something to drink and just have fun."

The captain replied, "I figured you had sense enough not to do that, but I can understand these boys wanting to get out and get wild. Damn it, when I send you ashore, I mean for you to stay on the beach. Now, go down and get cleaned up and go to work!"

I never will forget that captain. We turned around and as we started to walk off, the captain walked over and put his arm around me. He knew I was just a kid and he said, "Son, I want to tell you something. When I was your age, I would have done the same thing." He just laughed and walked away. I thought, "Damn, he's a nice guy."

SS Brig. Gen. Alfred J Lyon *in Palawan.*

John A. was becoming increasingly independent as his time in service continued, especially because of his being surrounded by older men who were skilled and grounded. He learned so much and was able to send money home to his family, which was always desperately needed.

> I thought I was the luckiest man on earth in everything I did. My parents could use the money, and I thought it was good I could send money home, to help feed them. I never considered that an obligation. I just considered they needed the money, so I used to give them most of my paycheck.

However, there was a time when John A. stopped writing letters home to his mother, much to the dismay of the captain who called him to the bridge to discuss it.

Momma would write me the worst letters you ever read. "If we had some money, I could get the boys a paper route, but they don't have a bicycle to carry it on." Bicycles only cost twenty dollars back then, so I sent her enough money for the bicycles. The letters depressed me so much, I just quit writing home altogether. I hadn't written in four months and my mother wrote to the ship administration in the War Department to see if something had happened to me.

One day I was on the ship in the Philippines and it came over the loud speaker. "John Hobbs, go to the captain's quarters." I thought, "Whoa hell, what have I done?" I went up to the captain's quarters and he said, "Sit down there. I want to know why you haven't written your mother in so long. I got a letter from the War Department wanting to know if you are still living. Son, you have to write your mother."

I said, "Well, if you read some of the letters I got, I don't believe you'd write home either."

"What are you talking about? Have you still got some of these letters?"

"Yes sir."

"Go get them."

I went downstairs and brought them back up there and placed four of them on his desk. He looked at each one and said, "My God. I don't blame you, because I wouldn't want to hear from them either." Every one of them was about how bad off the family was and what they needed. I just got to where I didn't want to hear any more.

The captain said, "I want you to write your mother, and I am going to censor your letter." During the war, the officers censored the letters on the ship where you couldn't tell where you were at, what you were doing, or anything about the war. So, I wrote Mom and told her that I was alright and doing good. I carried it up and gave the letter to the cap-

tain as promised. He censored it, and stamped it "approved".
"I am going to send this to your mother." I wrote a few more
times then quit again, but he never said anything else to me.

Always commanding a ship, General Douglas MacArthur
was the supreme commander in the Pacific and used the *USS
Nashville* as his flagship on several occasions. This new 608-foot
ship could reach 32.5 knots and was capable of an astounding
rate of fire. In fact, it had the greatest firepower of any treaty
cruisers of any country in the world.[16]

As the Allies island-hopped their way across the Pacific,
the *USS Nashville* was leading the pack. MacArthur brought his
wife, young son Arthur, and their nanny along with him. General
MacArthur's only son, Arthur MacArthur IV, was born in Manila
in 1938 and rarely spent time with his father despite traveling
together through the Pacific. The nanny would play with the boy
and serve as his teacher while away from school, but his father
was much too busy to spend any quality time with him. This
was a sad reality that would later cause their relationship to be
strained. The general moved the ship's entire crew to the bow,
leaving the stern primarily for the use of his family.[17]

General MacArthur's ship pulled up and anchored alongside the *SS Brig. Gen. Alfred J. Lyon*. With their respective ships
anchored so close to one another, John A., through field glasses,
could watch the "Big Chief" go ashore daily in the mornings and
return in the evenings.

We were anchored about a city block from General Douglas
MacArthur, leaving some room for our ships to swing with
the tide. We looked through the field glasses on the bridge to
watch him, and we could see him come and go from shore.
Every evening after supper, he'd sit up on deck and read. I

thought General MacArthur was an old man during the war, but he was only sixty-five. He looked old and I thought he was, but it was a different world. MacArthur would be sitting there smoking a large corn-cob pipe and reading a book. He never got up and played with his boy, but the nanny did, and his wife got up once in a while.

They awarded the Congressional Medal of Honor, the highest military honor America gives, to MacArthur's father, Arthur MacArthur, in World War I and to Douglas MacArthur in World War II. We never knew how he got it since he wasn't in the big battles. He might have been on the edge of the fighting, but he was never like General Patton, who was always right up there with them in the middle of everything. He was probably a good general, I don't know. There were things that we didn't understand. Things that were way above us.

CHAPTER NINE

Bombs Away

It is my earnest hope and indeed the hope
of all mankind that from this solemn occasion
a better world shall emerge out of the blood
and carnage of the past.

—GENERAL DOUGLAS MACARTHUR

The *SS Brig. Gen. Alfred J. Lyon* was anchored in Manila in August 1945, while its crew was preparing to invade Japan on September 8, 1945. The men busied themselves fitting all the ships with machine guns. It was presumed that Japanese soldiers would attempt to swim out to the ships, and they planned to shoot them in the water before they could make it.

> We had already been in the Pacific and fighting was still going on there when we dropped the first atomic bomb. I didn't know what an atomic bomb was—I never had even heard of it. We all found out pretty quick what it was. They figured we were going to lose countless lives in that invasion, so I was glad they dropped it.

The Manhattan Project, led by the United States, was a research and development project in Los Alamos, New Mexico.

SS Brig. Gen. Alfred J Lyon *in dry dock in Yokohama, Japan.*

It was at this national laboratory that scientific director and physicist J. Robert Oppenheimer led a large group of scientists who designed the atomic bomb used to end World War II. The nuclear weapon was designed for complete devastation with power evolving from the rapid release of nuclear energy created by fission of heavy atomic nuclei. Destruction is a result of the blast, which produces extreme heat and poisonous radioactivity. President Harry S. Truman made the most difficult decision of his life when he ordered the use of the "special bombs" on Japan.

The first atomic bomb, nicknamed "Little Boy," was dropped from the *Enola Gay*, a B-29 named after the mother of the plane's pilot, Col. Paul W. Tibbets. The approximately ten-thousand-pound bomb, dropped via parachute, exploded over the manufacturing center Hiroshima on August 6, 1945. The bomb destroyed more than five city miles, injuring and killing approximately 135,000 people. The bomb stopped the impending invasion of Japan, but not the war, with the Japanese refusing to surrender.[18]

Then there was the B-29 Bockscar, named after the original aircraft commander, Frederick C. Bock. For this mission, the Bockscar, piloted by Maj. Charles Sweeney, carried the second plutonium bomb, which bore the nickname "Fat Man."[19] This bomb was dropped on secondary target Nagasaki, Japan, on August 9, 1945. Heavy cloud covering had forced a move from the primary target of the city of Kokura to Nagasaki. Although the ten-thousand-pound bomb was more powerful than the bomb used on Hiroshima, the topography of Nagasaki dampened the bomb's effect, leading to a less substantial death toll of approximately forty thousand.

Together these weapons of mass destruction, the only nuclear weapons so far used in the history of warfare, forced the Japanese to surrender. Emperor Hirohito announced Japan's surrender via radio broadcast on August 15, 1945. For years to come, many would debate the necessity of using these weapons of mass destruction, but the estimated death toll of the invasion that ultimately never took place was well over one million lives.[20] Perhaps one of those lives lost would have been that of young John A. Hobbs. Fate would have it that he would live to tell about the surrender and one of the greatest displays of military might ever.

The war was officially over, but the treaty had yet to be signed in Tokyo Bay. The *SS Brig. Gen. Alfred J. Lyon* was the first supply vessel to enter Tokyo Bay. Its onboard Sikorsky R-4 helicopters helped evacuate the wounded and sick service men to the hospital ship nearby. Some of the evacuees came from the Bataan Death March, the forcible transfer by the Imperial Japanese army of thousands of Filipino and American prisoners of war. Many were forced to work in the coal mines for years, emerging as skin and bone, and blinded by the sunlight.[21]

> The representatives from the hospital ship asked us if we could come over and help them load, so we went over and helped in any way we could. We walked those that could walk and the ones that couldn't walk, we carried. As soon as it was loaded, the hospital ship left out for San Francisco, leaving us the only ship out there in the bay until the others started coming in.

On Sunday, September 2, more than two hundred fifty Allied warships were anchored next to them in Tokyo Bay. The *USS Missouri* hoisted the flags of the United States, Britain, the Soviet Union, and China. Japanese Foreign Affairs Minister Mamoru Shigemitsu signed on behalf of the government of Japan; General Yoshijiro Umezu signed for the Japanese armed forces; and General Douglas MacArthur signed on behalf of the United Nations.

> They signed the treaty in Tokyo Bay and were demonstrating just how much might the Americans had. We had to move our ship over and the *USS Missouri* went right by us and on up to the front to anchor. They had about twelve submarines and another ship out there, pulling the subs up on each

side of the *USS Missouri*. America brought in the whole third fleet, which was over at least two hundred ships. They flew planes over the day of the treaty. The B-29's flew over in formation, then came the B-17's, the B-24's, and the P-38's! We were all up on deck watching when they flew in formation right over our ship. They came out by barge and little destroyers brought them boys out.

We could watch it all; we were maybe two city blocks from it, and each ship was anchored where they could swing with the tide and not hit each other. They were so close together you thought you could throw a baseball over to them. I never knew we had that much might. There were five battleships and there must have been fifteen or twenty, large aircraft carriers and a lot of smaller carriers. There were all kinds of destroyers and everything else in there. I didn't know how much history I was really seeing because I was so young and didn't understand it all. I believe that MacArthur did do a remarkable job with Japan. They treated us well when we showed up, and I was shocked at my age how many people there could speak English. MacArthur treated them well and in return, they treated us well, but there was so much difference between the Japanese people in Tokyo and the soldiers that were fighting us. The Japanese soldiers were cruel, they were awful cruel, and we couldn't even write home about it.

The Second World War was behind them, but Mother Nature threw one last curveball at the Allied forces. On September 10, 1945, a typhoon slammed into the *SS Brig. Gen. Alfred J. Lyon* near Guam. In the 1940s, the technological capabilities to predict strong storms such as these mature tropical cyclones did not exist. The officers giving the orders to move had no idea what they were sending their men into, but waves a hundred feet high broke two ships apart, resulting in the loss of more than three thousand men.[22]

> The people that ordered us didn't know that storm was there. We all came up into the hallways and put on life jackets and helmets because we thought our ship would break in two.

CHAPTER TEN

Home Again

I guess I'd fight a circular saw in those days.
—JOHN A. HOBBS

John A. faithfully sent most of his allotment checks to his family, but when it came time for John A. to return home, he didn't have enough money to make the trip.

I thought they'd saved me a little bit of the money for when I got home, so I called up and said, "Mom, I don't have any money. I am coming home, but I need a little money to get home on."

She said, "Well, we don't have it."

I went in to the shipping department and told them I didn't have any money to get home because my pay was still in route from the United States to Japan. It was November, and I said, "I'd like to go home for Christmas." This Filipino man was there and he said, "Son, your pay won't get here for two weeks. I want to hurry it up, and I'll find out where it's at, but if you can make a trip down to Panama in the meantime, I'll have it for you when you get back."

So, I got on another ship and made the trip down to Panama and when I returned, he said, "I told you I'd get your money." He had it all there, and I made about four hundred additional dollars on that last excursion.

John A. took a freighter boat with approximately fifty other men toward San Francisco, but a change in orders sent the boat headed to Alaska. It was cold and they had shacks built on the deck with bunks in them and no heat, so John A. chose to sleep inside the ship on the floor, where it was heated from the steam. He just wanted to get home and didn't mind where he had to sleep to get there. It took almost two weeks to reach Seattle. Once there, he took the train to Chicago and on to New Orleans, and managed to make it home in time for Christmas. He hadn't been home in more than eighteen months, so it was a great surprise for his family when he pulled up out front in a cab on Christmas Eve, 1945. The end of his term of service was in sight, and he only had January and the first part of February 1946 left to serve before he could return home for good.

John A.'s run-ins with monumental figures in history continued with a chance meeting of the Galveston Giant, Jack Johnson, in New York City. Jack Johnson was an American boxer who at the height of the Jim Crow Era had become the first African American to win boxing's heavyweight title. He was wild in his day and controversial because of his marriages to white women. Observers of boxing such as writer Jack London called out for a Great White Hope to take away the title, but it never happened. John A. and Johnson's paths crossed in New York in 1946 just months before Johnson would be killed in a car accident in North Carolina.[23]

> We were in New York for a couple of weeks where they were working on our ship, getting it ready for a trip to Europe to transport war brides back to the United States. We went to a show every evening and returned to the ship late at night.
>
> One night, we were down off Fifth Avenue, just me and Ralph and two other guys, and they had a side show set up

in a big building down there. A big shop was set up down there in the basement where Jack Johnson was speaking. He was black, but he married white women, which was unheard of in the thirties. We were standing, and there were maybe fifty to seventy-five people, and I think it was a dollar and a quarter a head. It was his turn to get up and talk a little bit, but a couple of smart-ass boys from New York were heckling him. He would act real humble and didn't know what to do. So, I guess I'd fight a circular saw in those days. I went over and said, "You boys either shut up, or get out of here! Leave the man alone! He was the world heavyweight champion and he is a good man, and I don't think you have any business heckling him."

So, my boys, my friends, came with me. We were going to take them on, but they left. We stayed and listened to him speak and when he finished, Jack Johnson motioned for me to come over and said, "I want to thank you for takin' up for me." I told him, "I didn't mind it because I thought he was a good man."

"I married a white woman, and a lot of people hate me for it."

"That's between you and her," I replied.

We didn't stay long after that, but I was always glad I met him. He was old then, I guess he must have been maybe in his late sixties, but I know when he was younger, he was wild and did a lot of crazy stuff. Other than that, he was a pretty good fella. I was going to really make a career in the service, but I'll tell you what happened. We picked up a new ship at Norfolk and there were a lot of southern boys on it. Then we picked up a lot of black soldiers in New York. They put our ship in the Brooklyn Navy Yard to renew it. A brand-new one, and we were going to go to Europe. I had never been to Europe and I was looking forward to it.

I walked into the mess hall one morning and the whites were over here and the blacks were over there. I walked in, and I went over with the whites quickly because I didn't know what was going on. My buddy Ralph had a big cut across his throat and he said, "That's it, we'll commit a race riot right here!" The general alarm sounded and I never saw so many MPs, SPs, and police in my life. They took our ship out and anchored it in the Hudson River. They ordered everybody to their rooms and then made an announcement over the speaker system for all the southern boys that boarded in New Orleans to pack our bags and come up on deck. We were going to be shipped back to the South, and I hadn't even done anything. I didn't even know what it was all about when I walked in the mess hall that morning. We were put on boats that brought us back to New Orleans. It was really a race riot, that early, but I never knew the whole story of it.

The war was over in 1945, and after the race riot aboard the ship in New York, John A. returned home at age eighteen, in February 1946. It would be another forty-three years before he was reunited with some of his fellow shipmates in their first reunion held in Nashville. The last time the men would all be together while in uniform was in September 1945.

When I hosted the ship's first reunion here in Nashville in August of 1989, we had a lot of fun. It was held at the Rodeway Inn, one of the four hotels that we owned, and it was a big party. This was the first time in more than forty years we had all come together, and we had about two hundred fifty attend, including spouses. I asked all the Opry stars to come, and I thought maybe two or three would show up. You won't believe it, but every one of them came. Every Opry star I asked attended the event because they were all friends of mine. Roy Acuff, Jack Greene, Jeannie Seely, George Jones, and all the big stars. Just name them off back then and they all came to it, so I put one or two stars at each dinner table. They all asked me, "What do you want us to do?" I said, "Just eat and talk with them, maybe tell them a little bit about country music." Many of the stars got up on stage and performed for us. Johnny Russell sang his hit song, "Act Naturally." Jim Ed Brown sang and so did Jeannie Seely. Everyone got up on stage because they were World War II veterans and the guys couldn't believe it, they were so impressed. They said, "God, we didn't know you knew all these people." They couldn't get over it because I was the lowest man on the ship. They didn't get any lower than me. They all laughed and cut up about it, but we took good care of them, and they had a big time.

Geoffrey E. Ballard traveled three thousand miles by himself across the other side of Australia, then flew to Nashville just to be here. He came in for the reunion a day or two early, and we were all so glad to see him. The first night he was out with us at our Nashville Palace, Tom Powell was in there drinking like a fish. At one point, Tom fell out of his bar seat and onto the floor. This old man looked down at him and said, "Sonny, can't you hold your liquor?" I didn't know what to think, an eighty-year-old man asking if you can hold your liquor? We really got a kick out of that. A reunion book was created with everybody's name in it and their pictures, and it had a picture of me in uniform when I was sixteen years old on the front cover. They dedicated the entire reunion to me and wrote, "It is with great pleasure that we dedicate this book to John A. Hobbs. His great enthusiasm, drive, generosity, and foresight has made this reunion a tremendous success and an event that we will long remember." I thought that was so nice.

CHAPTER ELEVEN

Finding Love

*I just took every day for granted, but I thanked God
I had good health when I was young and for everything
that he did for me. Somebody had to help me,
I only had an eighth grade education.*

—JOHN A. HOBBS

ohn A. joined the war as a teenager and returned home a young man. He brought with him a tremendous amount of worldly education, and he tried to settle back into life in West Nashville. Despite his life experience, without a trade or a formal education past the eighth grade, he had no idea what he was going to do. It wasn't long before he landed a job in construction with a large company.

I went to work at Cartwright and Herman when I first came out of the service, making seventy-five cents an hour digging ditches. I learned a lot through watching the people I worked with. I figured if they could do that much, I could do a little bit of it and maybe even improve it. I didn't know how to dig a ditch, but there was a skill to it. I had the crookedest ditch to lay a pipe you ever did see. They all laughed and then showed me how to mark it and move the line out of the way. I learned something, how to get a straight ditch. There's a trick to even the lowest trade. I did that for a day or two and then my boss raised me up and put me in concrete work which was hard work.

I worked in my navy clothes, but I never was uniform crazy and never wore my uniform when I came home. I wore my civilian clothes to the skating rink and everywhere else. One old boy I went to school with named Johnny, who recently joined the navy, was kind of cocky. He was home on his first leave and thinking he was a big shot in his uniform, he said, "Hey Hobbs! Ain't it about time for you to go in the service?"

I looked at him and said, "Johnny, I've already been in."

"Where did you go?"

I started naming off the islands I had been to: Kwajalein, Palawan, Leyte, Luzon, Eniwetok, Palau, and he said, "I didn't know you were out there."

"I just got back the day before yesterday."

"Well, I'll be damned!"

John A. had been home only a few weeks before he connected with a childhood acquaintance who would change the course of his life. John A. and his best friend Pat Mitchell were hanging out at Shirley's, a popular little ice cream parlor, when Mary Kittrell caught their eye driving into the parking lot in her 1940 Ford with girlfriend Martha McGill.

Mary and John A., circa 1946.

She was setting up in front of Shirley's with Martha and they said, "Y'all wanna race?"

I said, "Will your car hit a hundred miles an hour?"

"Yeah!"

"Well, I'll save you from racing. Let's just ride in yours."

Pat Mitchell was with me, and we went over to the car and got to talking to them. Mary said, "We can go over to another place, get in!" So, me and Pat got in the back seat and they started to back out of the parking lot.

I said, "This is funnier than hell, two men in the back and two women in the front. Don't you think one of you ought to be back here?"

Mary stopped the car and got in the back seat with me, and Pat got in the front with Martha. We went over to Ace Barbecue on White Bridge Road in West End and ordered beer. We weren't old enough to drink, but the waiters brought it to you anyway. After that, we started going out and we had a lot of fun. Martha's father was the warden at The State Penitentiary on the lower farm, and they wanted us to go horseback riding with them on the prison farm.

We would go on hayrides, and the inmates wrote songs and would walk behind the plodding wagon playing music for us. We were living it up down there, and we were dating and having a lot of fun going out. A friend of mine had just come home from the navy and started dating a girl named Shirley. One night he said, "Johnny, we need to get married and settle down here. We're killing ourselves running every night. If you'll get married, I'll get married!"

I agreed, and so we asked our girls to marry us. Two other couples decided they would get married at the same time, so I borrowed my Aunt Nellie's 1937 Ford to drive us the forty-five miles to the courthouse in Franklin, Kentucky. It was a required three-day waiting period in Nashville, but in

John A. visiting The State Penitentiary Farm, circa 1945.

Franklin you simply had to get a blood test and then you could get married right away. We had four couples piled in that car, and they were sitting on each other's laps. We hit a hill and the car wouldn't pull up it because it only had sixty horsepower, so I turned the car around and backed it up.

When we arrived, two people changed their minds, but we got married August 9, 1946, the anniversary date of when they dropped the second atomic bomb one year before. We had nothing and we started out with nothing. Mary was seventeen years old, and I was eighteen. I didn't even have civilian clothes and was wearing my navy Dungaree outfits for work until my Aunt Nellie gave me fifteen dollars to buy me a dress pair of pants and a shirt I could get married in. We went down to Ashland City, to the mouth of the Harpeth River, and camped there that weekend for our honeymoon.

We had a big time down there, but boy after that, I really had to buckle down. Mary got pregnant on the honeymoon and I thought, "Good God, how am I going to feed a baby? I can't even feed us!" Our first son, Michael Anthony was born May 11, 1947 at Vanderbilt Hospital and I didn't know what we were going to do. It's really the

Pat Mitchell, Mary Kittrell, and John A. Hobbs, circa 1945.

truth, if you don't have a helping hand, you can't go anywhere. My life has been good to me, but hard when I was a kid. After I was grown, the first ten years were hard, I was working my ass off. I could see that I wanted to be somebody and to make a good living, and I worked at it every day.

Gatlinburg: Yvonne and Pat Mitchell, Mary and John A. Hobbs, circa 1950.

With new baby Michael, they moved in with Mary's mother on Robinson Road until they could rent a house of their own. It was tough times, and John A. understood how important it was to keep his construction job, so he worked beyond expectations to impress his boss, John Cartwright. One day Cartwright came out on the job and told John A. to pick up a saw and a few hand tools, because he had been promoted to carpenter.

> They gave me a break, knowing I was a hard worker. We were building a house across the street from my boss, John Cartwright. I didn't know this until later in life, but my boss and his mother-in-law would watch us work from the window. I would run and pick up two or three boards at a time and stand them up against the building then run around to the other side. I really ran while I was working because I was afraid I'd get fired, and we were really having a hard time.

CHAPTER TWELVE

Taking Risks

If you know what you're worth,
you're not worth much.
—JACK MASSEY

John A. continued his upward movement within the company and eventually reached the lead position as foreman. He worked hard for his pay and wasn't afraid to speak up when his paycheck wasn't the amount he thought he deserved.

First house John A. built in West Nashville for his family.

> When it came time for payday, I told my boss that I thought I would get a little more money. He walked up to me and said, "Did you like the raise we gave you?"
>
> Surprised, I said, "I didn't get any raise."
>
> "Really? You were supposed to, I told them to give you one."
>
> "Well, I didn't get it."
>
> "You'll have it next week!"
>
> He left and his partner Mark Herman came up to me and asked, "Are you satisfied with your raise?"
>
> I said, "No, I didn't get a raise."
>
> "Well, we will take care of that."
>
> The next week I received a good, healthy raise as promised.

As one of their final projects, the construction company built a large hotel in Nashville. John A. was foreman overseeing the massive project and coordinating the onsite workers. When the project was finished, the partners offered John A. an opportunity they were hoping he would jump at. They wanted him to run this new hotel for them, and they sweetened the deal with a hefty raise that made for a solid salary. This new direction was tempting for a young man with a growing family, but John's internal compass wouldn't let him settle for being stuck running a hotel. He dreamed of one day building his own hotels and accomplishing much more than that with his life, so he graciously turned them down. He immediately took his talents to one of the largest builders in Nashville, Evans and Morris.

> They were building two thousand houses at a time, but the company was splitting. Dave Crockett was their foreman, so he was going in partnership with E. S. Evans and he was working a hundred-fifty men when I went over there.
>
> He took me in and asked, "What do you do?"
>
> I replied, "I can do a little bit of everything in building."

"Can you hang wall paper?"

"No, I've never hanged any wall paper."

"Good! I'll hire you because I don't want no wallpaper hanger!"

He laughed and he was a good guy, and they liked me.

So, we went to work and I got along good.

In fact, Mr. Crockett and John A. got along very well and stayed friends until Crockett died from a heart attack while in his sixties. Dave Crockett was a good man, a smart builder, and he took the time to educate John A. in all aspects of building. Having only one daughter of his own as well as several step-daughters, Mr. Crockett brought John A. under his wing and treated him like the son he had always wanted.

Within three years of starting, John A. moved up to foreman, running the jobs and doing everything for the company. With his family growing with the birth of his second son, Joe, he bought a lot from his mother for five hundred dollars and began building his own two-room house in West Nashville. He worked nonstop on it, but when it was finished, he was so proud of it.

First, I built one bedroom and the kitchen with an outside toilet. When we moved in, I started two more rooms and a bath. It took me three months to build it, working at night and on the weekends. A lot of the guys I worked with would come by and help me for an hour or two, but we were all working ten hours a day, six days a week. and then I was building a house for myself on the side.

You wouldn't believe it, but I built that house for less than three thousand dollars and only had five hundred in the lot. The only problem was that we lived next door to my mother, and I thought, "Oh, Lord, I made a bad mistake, we don't need to be living here." I was ready to build my own house out there in Donelson and move from West Nashville, because I could see there was no future for us. The people were all poor people, having a hard time, living in shacks. I thought, "We need to get out of here." I put the house up for sale and sold it for seventy-five hundred dollars and bought a lot in Donelson for seventeen hundred and fifty dollars.

Albert Morris, a big developer and a good friend of mine, called me up one day and invited me to his office for a cup of coffee. He was really fair and he said, "They tell me you want to buy a lot off me? I haven't sold a single one of them yet and we have four hundred-plus lots. Here's the plot plan, go out and pick you one out, and come back and see me. Any lot at cost, seventeen hundred and fifty dollars."

I went out there and walked them, then went in and showed him the lot I wanted. He asked, "Are you buying it for those shade trees?"

I said, "Yes, they're beautiful!"

"I am glad you picked that one out. It's a good lot with ninety feet across the front and a hundred and fifty-feet deep. Tell you what you do, don't pay me for the lot right now. I am going to put it in your name and when you get your permanent loan, let me know, and we'll just put the amount on there. You can just owe me until you get the house built."

I said, "Thanks a million, Albert!"

He put it in my name and when I got the house about finished, Dave asked, "Have you secured your loan yet?"

"No," I replied.

So, he called the bank here in town where his buddy was the vice president and told them, "Take care of Johnny Hobbs. I am sending him down there and he's a personal friend, so don't put any extra money on it." They gave me a loan with no brokerage fees at three and a half percent interest. I put a house on it and when I got through, I had to borrow three thousand dollars. My note was thirty-nine dollars a month and I thought, "How am I going to pay that?" I was really scared, but the house next door was selling for twelve thousand and mine was just as big and built much better. When we moved in, my mother came out to see it. She lost a house to the bank in 1933, and she said, "Oh, my God, you'll lose this house! There's no way you can pay for it!" I thought, "Oh, my God I am in enough trouble already."

CHAPTER THIRTEEN

Honest Day's Pay

A fifteen-dollar set of wood bits,
a half a pint of Jack Daniel's whiskey,
and a hundred dollars.
—JOHN A. HOBBS

ohn A. earned a decent wage while continuing to work for Evans and Morris. More importantly, he was learning life lessons that were worth their weight in gold. These were important lessons, like how to treat others with respect, standing up for yourself, and always being honest and straightforward. When John A. turned people down, they were never mad at him; they respected him and ran after him even more.

> I always wanted to treat a man like he treats me, never like an animal. I was doing a job as foreman, building a big warehouse. We worked hard on it and lacked maybe an hour and a half to finish, but it was already five thirty on a Friday night. The guy said, "I want to get it dried in tonight and get the felt on it where it won't get wet. If you will continue to work on it, I am going to give you a bonus."

We stayed and finished it that night, and the man took money out and threw it on the roof, letting the workers fight over it. I didn't pick any of the money up and just walked off. He asked, "You don't need money?" I looked him in the eye and said, "Yeah, but I don't have to dig like a dog," and walked off. You know he offered me a job after that saying, "Johnny, you could do good in the electrical business. Would you come in as a partner? I am starting another company, and I'll give you half interest in it."

"I don't want to be an electrician. I enjoy building, but I don't want to be stuck in the electrical business. I've got more in life I want to do."

"Well, you'd be a good electrician and you'd make money."

"I'd just rather not, but thank you."

He said, "I knew from the start you were going to do good. You are pretty level-headed and know how to handle business. Plus, you're not a smart-ass with people, you just go ahead and do it."

John A. learned something from everyone he knew. He learned different things from different people, and it really helped him throughout his life. He would simply watch others work and think to himself, "What they are doing is a good idea, but let's see how I can improve it."

I never looked at a clock, but one day we were building houses over on Crossville Drive in Donelson; I was running the job and I broke my watch. I knew there was a plane that flew over the houses every day, and landed at the nearby airport right at five o'clock. So, when the plane flew over, I knocked the men off, thinking it was quitting time. Turns out I let them go ten minutes early. The boss had driven up in his Cadillac and was sitting there smoking a cigar, just watching. He tapped his horn and motioned for me to come over there. We loaded up the trucks, and I walked over to his car.

He calmly asked, "How many men you got working on this job?"

I said, "About sixty."

"Sit down in the car here with me a minute. Let's say you give ten minutes to each one of them, times sixty." He paused and said, "You see what you cost me today? Never quit them early, always quit them right on time."

He took his watch off and said, "Here, take this damn watch! I know you don't have one now, and you may never get it fixed, so just keep it!"

I put it on and wore it, and I made sure from then on, I'd let them work ten minutes overtime and then say, "Alright, time to quit."

Mary was raising three boys now, Mike, Joe, and Ronnie. John A. was working harder than ever. It seemed the harder he worked, the more money the company made off him. Dave Crockett and his partner sent John A. to Clarksville to oversee 120 men building nearly sixty-five houses. During work on the project, Dave Crockett went down with a pulled muscle in his back, and with his partner off to Europe, the entire project was left up to John A.

I was so young and the workers were so old, I almost had to fight one every day because they thought they knew every-thing and I didn't know shit!

Clarksville was approximately fifty-five miles away, so once the first house was built, John A. moved in it and stayed through the week, where he could keep an eye on the project at night. Time sheets had to be turned in and the men paid, so he asked

Mary for help. She would go by the office, pick up the paychecks, and drive them to Clarksville every Friday morning.

We started building those houses, and Dave didn't come back for about three months. When he finally made it back down there, he said, "John, you did a good job!" Well, right away, I thought I would get a two or three-thousand-dollar bonus. Since I started with the company, I was given two raises and got up to a dollar and a quarter an hour, so that was good money. I thought, "Well, I'll get a big bonus at Christmas this year because they made a lot of money in Clarksville."

On Christmas Eve, Dave came out on the job where we were building a custom house, and do you know what he gave me? A fifteen-dollar set of wood bits, a half a pint of Jack Daniel's whiskey, and a hundred dollars. When he left, I looked at that and it was bitter cold that Christmas Eve. I thought, "My God. I ran the job for them and thought I would get something out of it, but I didn't." We had a fire going out back and I said, "Come on, boys! Get ready, we're going to knock off, and then time in for a full day. Open that bottle up and everybody take a drink. It's all I got." I told myself, "Well, I won't be here next year." I could see the writing on the wall, I wasn't going to get much out of it, and they bought two new Cadillacs.

That summer came along and Dave came to me. He already had a partner, but he told me, "Johnny, if I ever went into business with another man, I'd want you to be my partner. I would rather have you than anybody I know because me and you could really do some things."

I said, "Well, Dave, I appreciate that, but I am leaving you this year and going into business for myself."

He didn't look surprised and said, "I always knew someday you would do this because I knew that you had the ability to do it. I've always told people that you will either be rich or broke. I don't know which it will be, but you are a hard worker. I'll help you every way that I can."

He did always help me, and we never bid against each other on jobs. Now, I thank God, he didn't give me two thousand dollars that night, because I probably would have stayed with him.

CHAPTER FOURTEEN

Popping Bricks

Any man says, I made it on my own, is a damn liar.
You've got to have a lot of friends and a lot of help.
I had a lot of people that helped me in business
when I first went into it for myself.
—JOHN A. HOBBS

In 1957, at the age of twenty-eight, John A. went into business for himself starting the John A. Hobbs Construction Company. He was so young that people were afraid to give him a house to build, but he managed to keep busy with a regular stream of add-ons and remodeling. Fortunately, all the people he had worked with remained friends, and they all helped him.

I've learned from watching other people because I didn't have the education. When I first went into business, I couldn't afford to lose because I had no money to back me. I didn't want a partner, but everyone helped me. In fact, we did really well because they all helped me. Everybody has to have a lot of friends, especially if you are in business. I've heard a lot of men say, "I am a self-made man; I made it all myself." Well, he's telling you a damn lie because you've got to have people who know and help you to establish a business. I was lucky I had a lot of help from people, so I stayed busy and never lost any time going into business for myself.

Albert Morris was one of the largest contractors in Nashville building several thousand houses at one time. He took John A. in like family and help him get established by funneling extra business his way.

Albert would say, "Let the boy have the job, and he'll treat you right." They didn't even ask me a price, but I would build for them and when we got through, I'd put a profit on it and never had any arguments. I always tried to do a job like it was for me. I wanted things perfect. I had two or three men with me all my life on every job. The carpenter would say, "Ah, they won't notice that," and I'd say, "Don't leave it like that, it looks like hell," and we would straighten up whatever it was. So, you have to get on them and say, "Let's do it right." It doesn't take but a few minutes longer to do it right than to do it wrong and cut corners. There are ways that you can cut and save money, doing it right the first time is one of them. When I first went into business, I wasn't the guy that went out there and thought I knew everything in God's world, because I didn't. When I made a bad mistake, I'd say, "Woo, Lord, I could have gone to college for a year on that one, I'm not going to do that anymore." So, you learn from experience of what happened to you before and don't let it happen again. The first time is ignorance; the second time is stupidity.

Like anyone else, John A. managed to run into a few questionable characters while conducting business, but he always went straight to the heart of the issue, never mincing words.

Now, all my friends kid me saying, "Boy, you don't pull any punches when you're talking to people." I said, "Well, I don't believe in talking about somebody behind their back. If you're going to talk about anyone, talk to their face and try to help instead of hurting them."

I took my first big remodeling job out by Centennial Park. This guy ran a country club here in Nashville and I went out there, bid the job, and got it. When I began construction, a plumber came by that knew the owner and wanted the work. I didn't give him the job and instead called up a friend of mine and had him do the plumbing. One night, after my plumber had already finished the job, I was at home eating dinner and the phone rang. This guy called me up yelling, "What do you mean, giving them the job? I wanted to do that project because they are personal friends of mine!"

I said, "Well, they didn't tell me and I go by the cost. Your cost is too high and I needed to cut it, so I gave the job to someone else."

He threatened, "I'll tell you one thing, I'll cut off your loans and put you out of business!"

I said, "How are you going to cut it off? I don't have any money borrowed, and I am operating on my own money right now." I got mad and asked, "Where are you at?"

"I am in my office."

I said, "Stay there!"

I slammed the phone down, got up from the table and took off in my truck. I never will forget, I had a ten-dollar bill rolled up into a little ball in my hand as I was getting in, I threw it in the bed of the truck and forgot about it. I drove the truck on over to that plumbing shop and went into the middle of a meeting he was having with a guy running for sheriff. When he saw me, he said, "Ah, Johnny, how are you doing?'

I just said, "Let's talk!"

"He's a friend of mine, so go ahead and say anything you want to."

"Well, let me tell you something! I believe in talking to a man face-to-face, and I am telling you, I don't have any money borrowed. I don't owe a bank anything! I am paying for it myself and I am struggling, but I am making it! I don't appreciate what you said and I'll tell you right now, I don't believe you're big enough to put me out of business!"

He backed down and said, "Ah, I didn't mean that. I am just hot-headed and only wanted to do that job because I knew the owners."

"Well, you hit the wrong fella, because you'll never do a damn thing for me!"

I walked out and thought, "Now what did I do with that money?" I looked in the bed of the truck and that thing was still rolled up. I got it out, put it in my pocket, and drove off. I went straight to him because I don't believe in going through anybody. Just go out there and tell him what you think, and if you want to fight, then let's fight. People like that were one of the downfalls and I ran into a lot of people that were different. Some of them thought they were smart and had a lot of money and didn't. Those are the ones you have to watch out for. There's a lot of heisters in this world that want to live off you, if you'll do the work.

John A. will tell you that in the construction business you must be a psychiatrist, a judge, a doctor, and a decorator, telling people what they want and knowing what they don't want, but most importantly, you must have the right people working with you. Ninety-nine percent of the time he was working for a good family that had two or three kids and needed more room. That's the way he found business—through other families that would recommend his work, and he never had to advertise very much.

John A. did a lot of work for some of the wealthiest people in Nashville, building his business on the premise that he would take care of anything that went wrong.

I built a house one time for a one-armed guy that secured a farm loan. I never did ask him how he lost his arm, but I went out to the site with a friend of mine to get the figures, put in the lowest bid, and got the job building this house. I was doing good with it, but the closer we got to finishing, the slower he was paying me. I finished and I was taking my family to Florida for vacation. I had them all get ready that morning while I went to pick my check up at his house. I went out there around nine-thirty and he gave me my check. I headed straight for the bank, but he had already stopped payment on it. I called my wife and said, "Mary, we can't go to Florida. I hate to disappoint you, but I have troubles on the job and have to stay here another day or two."

I went back out to his house, picking up my long-time friend and worker, Buster, along the way. I warned him that I may hit this man. I am going to put one hand behind my back and if he hits me, and whips my ass, it's okay. Just let him hit me. I want him to swing at me, then I am going to swing with my left hand. I won't hit him with my right one, but I am going to fight him with one arm.

I confronted the man telling him, "The bank has already cleared this job. The Farmer's Bank in Gallatin said it was a fine home and well-built."

He said, "Well, the bricks are 'popping' on it!" (When you have new bricks, the small particles of lime located near the surface swell with absorbed moisture and cause pieces of the brick face to "pop" off.)

I said, "Let's go out there," and he walked right up close to the bricks. I said, "That isn't the way you do that! You have to examine the bricks from farther away to get a better idea of the quality of the workmanship and product Just wait here a minute."

I went to the truck and called in and had the brick company send a salesman out right away. When the brick salesman came over to the house, I said, "Tell me what's wrong with these bricks, because you guaranteed them."

He said, "Fella, you stand back twenty feet to look at an all-brick spot, you can't go up and pick out the ones that are 'popping.' Stay back twenty feet and look at them and if it looks bad all over, we will tear it down and replace it. There's nothing wrong with these bricks, they are in good shape."

I said, "I tried to tell him that."

Buster and I were still standing there, and the sales rep said, "Look, Johnny. I am gone, but I'll furnish you a lawyer, if that's what it takes. Let him sue or whatever he wants to do, but you got a case and we'll back you up 100 percent."

This guy walked back into his basement, thinking he was really smart, so I got so mad at him. I took my right hand and put it behind my back in my belt and I walked over to him. I said, "I am going to tell you something; you're a rotten, good-for-nothing, and I am calling you a good-for-nothing because you are rotten! I was taking my family to Florida this morning and you broke their hearts. I've got one hand behind my back and I am going tell you one thing before I leave here. I am either going to whip your ass, or I am going to get me a new check. We can call the police and let them settle it, but by God, I want my money!"

He yelled, "I'll get it! I'll get it! I'll get it! I am going to write you another one right now!"

He went upstairs, wrote me a check for the balance owed, brought it back down and handed it to me. I drove it to the bank, and they cleared it this time. A few days later, the bank called me and asked, "Johnny, What's wrong with that man? There's nothing wrong with that house."

I said, "I don't ever want to see that bastard again, he's crazy. He's trying to get something for nothing." I ran into him a couple of times at a local restaurant and just ignored him. I told my wife one time, "I knew that man years ago, I wanted to whoop his ass then and I still do! I wish he had two arms, so I could."

CHAPTER FIFTEEN

His Own
Boss

I'd just rather go on like I am going.
I like being my own boss and working
to make my own business successful.
—JOHN A. HOBBS

Partnership offers were plentiful, but although some were very tempting, John A. didn't waver from his desire to be his own boss. He held his ground even when pressured by his good friend, Albert Morris, who was one of the largest builders in the city. Morris was building a new subdivision called Murray Heights, and he wanted John A. to partner with him on it. One morning, while visiting over a strong cup of coffee in his office, Albert pulled out the blueprints for the expansive Murray Heights project in an attempt to woo a partnership with John A.

> Albert said, "Now, Johnny. I've got all these lots right here, and I want you to go over and pick you out about ten lots. You and I are going to become partners on these houses. I'll keep the books, put up the lots and all the investment money. I am

going to pay you a salary for working out there, and we're going to split the profit at the end. You won't be out any of your own money, and you will have the books to look at any time you want."

I knew he was a friend and a straight shooter, but I said, "Whoa, whoa, wait a minute, Albert. You hit me too fast! It's a good thing, but I don't know if I want to do that."

He said, "okay, then when can you let me know?"

I told him that I would have an answer for him tomorrow.

"Great! Think about it and I'll see you tomorrow."

I worried about it all day and had a sleepless night thinking, "Boy, it's a chance for me to really get going big, but I really don't want a partner."

The next morning, I got up, shaved, and ate breakfast. I said to myself, "He's like an old maid; he'll be calling me every night, wanting to know what I was doing, what was going on and I don't want to get back into that."

I went back to his office first thing that morning to tell him. He smiled and said, "Well, what did you come up with?"

I said, "Albert, I believe in being honest with a man and telling him what you think. I appreciate the offer. It's a hell of a good offer, but I want to be in business for myself. I am just going to shoot straight here. I really don't want a partner. You're kind of like an old maid; you'd be calling me every night, wanting to know what I was doing and what was going to happen tomorrow. I'd just rather go on like I am going. I like being my own boss and working to make my own business successful."

He was disappointed and said, "I don't blame you, but you can't blame me either. I knew me and you could make some good money together."

We remained friends until his death, and we loved to cut up and kid with each other. I never will forget going to his office one day, and he was eating a barbecue ham sandwich. We were always kidding each other, cutting up and laughing.

He said, "I understand your brother got a divorce?"

I said, "Yeah, he got one last month."

"I didn't think Catholics got divorced?"

I said, "I didn't think Jews ate pork, either?"

He started laughing and said, "Well, I am a reformed Jew."

For only having an eighth grade education, I was very lucky in life and in business.

John A. made great money back when he was in his forties, and a lot of money in his lifetime with all of his business endeavors. He now had four sons with the birth of little Johnny Conroy Hobbs, thirteen years after Ronnie. The family was still living in that little, three-bedroom house John A. had built in Donelson. There was a bedroom downstairs with a big den, which made it nice and comfortable. Mary was more attached to it than he realized. Always thinking ahead, John A. purchased two lots next to each other in the late seventies for ten thousand dollars apiece and planned to build a much larger new home for his family.

I didn't tell Mary that I had bought these two lots because I wanted to fill in the low spots and make them look good before taking her over to see them. I put Mary in the truck one day and I said, "Let's ride in the truck. I want to show you two lots we own." I said, "Mary, this is a beautiful place right here to build. There are higher-priced homes from where we are at and I'll build a nice three- or four-bedroom house right here and it will be on one level. You won't have to walk up and down the steps or anything." I told her that I was going to let her design it and everything, but she wasn't happy. She said, "I am not moving! I like my neighborhood, I like my neighbors and I am staying where I am at, but you can move

> if you want to. Now, let's go home!" My heart sank and I said, "Mary, you know I am not going to move over here without you." We went back home, and I kept the lots maybe two or three months and turned around and sold the lots for forty thousand dollars apiece.

With each passing year, the once-happy couple started drifting apart and the relationship became strained under the pressure of the difficulties. Mary was simple and much more reserved than John A., preferring a crossword puzzle at home over attending important business functions with her husband. This proved to be the breaking point and after thirty-five years of marriage, they divorced in 1981. Accepting most of the blame, he still admits that Mary was a wonderful mother and continued to make certain she was always well taken care of up to the time of her death on August 6, 2017.

> Mary never read a book, never did anything. I am not condemning her, we were just young when we married and she took things the wrong way. We didn't argue in front of the kids,

Mike, John A., Mary, Joe, Ronnie, and, in front, Johnny C. Hobbs.

but sometimes she would get mad and we wouldn't talk for a year, unless it was about the boys. Mary later confessed to me saying, "It took me a long time to figure out what happen to us. We were so happy in our younger days, but Johnny, you moved ahead and I stood still. You always read and tried to learn things, but I never advanced and you did. You just went off and left me, at least that's the way it seemed to me." I've learned a lot from friends and from all the places that I've been. The day you quit learning, you are ready for a grave. I am eighty-nine now, and I still learn something new every day.

John A. has been a good father and strived to instill the same work ethic, morals, and values in his four sons. As each one of his boys turned thirteen years old, John A. customarily took them out on the job to work and learn with Buster, an old black man who had worked with him for years. Buster was a hard worker and highly skilled at his trade, taking his shovel and cutting the straightest ditch you ever looked at. Using leverage, he could put a large drainage pipe in without using a crane, and he trained the boys in the art of digging ditches.

This wise man educated each of the boys. When it came time for little Johnny, Buster said, "Mr. Johnny, do you want me to take him out and let him work with me?" John A. wanted Buster to show his sons everything, but most importantly, make them work. Buster made them work at a slow and steady pace, and they all put in a good day's worth of work. John A. grew up believing that daily work never killed anyone and was proud to see his boys all working. Unfortunately, Buster developed type 2 diabetes and later had to have his legs amputated.

Old Buster never could learn to walk on those artificial legs. He'd fall down and couldn't get back up, so he got a wheelchair and went everywhere in it. One morning I got tickled. My second wife, Libby was getting out all of these socks to give to Buster.

I said, "Libby, he doesn't have legs."

She said, "Oh, my God, I forgot about that!"

I used to visit and take him a hundred dollars and a fifth of whiskey. One time, I went down to visit him and noticed a bottle of whiskey in his room. I said, "Who gave you the whiskey?"

He said, "Joe brought it to me."

Joe was bringing him stuff, and all my boys would go by and see him and bring him things. They all liked him because he was nice to them and helped them when they were just kids. He was a good worker, and, Lord, he was a fine man.

CHAPTER SIXTEEN

Business Partners for Life

You know in business, it's like rolling dice.
When you roll a pair of dice, you're gambling
whether you're going to win or lose. In business,
you're gambling the same way. You have to win
more than you lose in decision making.
—JOHN A. HOBBS

Throughout your life there are certain people you can work with because things simply click between the two of you. John A. finally found such a business partner in Louis McRedmond. With Louis, he made an exception to his own number-one rule of only being in business for himself.

John A. and Louis McRedmond met at Holy Rosary Catholic Church, where they both attended mass. Like John A., Louis was a good man, and the two of them were very close, almost like brothers. They worked well together because they each had their own individual endeavors, aside from what they went in on together. John A. had his own successful construction company, and a liquor store, and Louis ran a prosperous rendering plant that he and his brother Pat founded in 1932. In the 1950s the family-owned business was incorporated as McRedmond Brothers, and even to this day, the descendants of Louis McRedmond manage the company in the same office located on the McRedmond Farm off of Massman Drive. The main function of the plant was the buying and selling of the by-products of the meat-packing industry, then cooking it up to make grease out of it. The products produced were used as ingredients in many different animal feeds. In addition to the rendering plant, Louis also owned several trucking companies and was very well off. If John A. had the idea, then Louis was for it, and together they made a lot of money and produced a great deal of change in that valley.

Thirteen-acre triangle of development at I-40 and Briley Parkway. The Rodeway Inn and Fiddler's Inn South.

The McRedmond brothers owned a rendering plant and, boy, it smelled like hell down there. Let me tell you, I went down there and built them a new plant that was way bigger than what they had. So, I had a crew down there working and they were still rendering cows and stuff over there, smelled awful. I had a young kid working with us and it was time to eat lunch. He said, "I am going over there out of the way to eat." He went over away from us and picked up a lid on a container and there was a dead dog inside the thing. He started throwing up and claimed he had to go home and left. We all just laughed. They had dead cows and horses brought in on the conveyor belt, and they skinned and cooked them. It was an awful business, but he had a lot of workers in there and did really well with it.

The landslide of motel businesses began one day in the 1950s when twenty-eight-year-old John A. was on the job site, building a house in Donelson. Mike Walsh came by to see if he was interested in going into business with him. Mike explained to John A. that his wife's uncle, Mr. Strausser, was a farmer who owned several hundred acres of property in a prime location. Mike had an idea to build an open-air market on it and was hoping they could get some of the land at a reasonable price to build it on. John A. had built a house for Mike in the past and thought he knew him well, so he agreed to a partnership on a parcel of land.

John A. and Mike didn't waste any time, heading straight over to the Uncle's house to discuss it further and find out just how much he wanted for it. The thirteen acres of property were in a busy location right where I-40 crosses Briley Parkway, near the main city airport. The uncle was willing to sell some of it and wanted sixty-seven thousand dollars for thirteen acres. Although there was a large mound of dirt that had to be removed before they could start building on it, John A. and Mike said they would buy it. Uncle Strausser insisted that he didn't want to be paid in cash for the land. He wanted a payment plan and property in trade. He agreed to transfer the land into Mike's and John A.'s names in exchange for payments every six months in a trust to the bank so he didn't have to pay taxes on it until the debt was paid off, plus ownership of a ten-thousand-dollar house in Donelson as down payment.

It wasn't long after the uncle transferred the land out of his name that he tried to have Mike and John A. sell it back to him, fearing that the delay in building something meant they were in danger of losing the property. John A. could see the potential from the beginning and declined to sell the property back to Uncle Strausser, knowing that it would be a good location to build a motel, which was one of his dreams in building—to construct and own a motel of his own. Unlike building a home, building a motel can take several years to construct with feasibility studies, planning, financing, codes, and permits, so the "delay" was very normal. Like most partnerships, John A. and Mike had opposing opinions on what should go on the land. Mike was anxious to build something immediately such as an open-air market, but John A. wanted a motel because there weren't any out there, and it would be a good spot to build one. He believed that the open-air market would be like a farm, where you must be there all the time overseeing it. It takes a while to plan and build a motel, and Mike was getting impatient.

There were other developers attempting to woo them into business and out of sole ownership of the prime property, but John A. wasn't having any of it. He told these heisters to match their original investment dollar-for-dollar and then they could be partners. They told him that they wanted John A. and Mike to put up the land and then they would borrow the land and build on it. John A. had the idea and the property, and he wasn't going to let anyone cheat him out of it. Against Mike's wishes, John A. refused to bring in these other partners: they now wanted to sell and get a big profit out of the land. About that time, a man from Kansas City, who owned two motels, wanted to build a motel on the property. He put up some money, and they went into partnership with him, but John A. soon realized he was going to try to root them out because he didn't need them. He called up Louis McRedmond and told him how he envisioned a better moneymaking scenario with a motel. Louis agreed that a motel would be a better investment than a drive-up market and wondered if Mike was willing to sell out to him, clearing the way for the motel and for a remarkable partnership that would last forty profitable years.

> We called Mike and he agreed to sell Louis McRedmond his share of the property for fifty thousand dollars, which was a good profit for Mike, but he sold at the wrong time. We went over to Mike's house that night to seal the deal, but couldn't find anything to write on except a sack. I wrote out a "Bill of Sale" on a paper sack not knowing whether it was legal or not. Louis bought him out, and he and I became partners on our first project.

> My partnership with Louis worked out so good, that we never had a cross word or argument. We never disagreed and always discussed everything, working it all out. If I wanted to close a deal, I'd say, "I have to run it by Louis," and if he wanted a deal, he'd say, "Johnny's got to approve this, too." Then we could work it out later and not have to do it in front of them. We had a good leverage that way. We were

John A. and Louis McRedmond placing hand and foot prints in concrete in Music Valley.

in business together for forty years, and that little corner we bought when I was twenty-eight years old, made us over three million dollars each.

The Scottish Inns of America chain began in Tennessee in the late 1960s. The company owned the hotels, which were modular type facilities constructed with an emphasis on budget accommodations. The Scottish Inns did not operate its own motels, but rather leased out the name. Louis and John A. built a two-story, garden-style motel with a restaurant in it and worked with the CEO of Scottish Inns, Charlie Scott, for the franchise name.

The economy-driven Scottish Inns was charging $8.95 per room per night. John A. was certain that he was in a location where he could charge more and make more money. So, in the early 1980s, he began asking and getting $12.50 per room per night. Charlie Scott found out about the rate hike and came out to discuss it with John A. personally. He told him that he would have to stay with the franchise pricing that is set, despite the favorable location. He reiterated that their original agreement was that the rooms would sell for the $8.95 per room per night and nothing more. He threatened to pull the franchise, but John A. insisted that there was no signed agreement between them, and to make money they would have to charge the additional monies. The next day, Charlie Scott pulled his Scottish Inns franchise signs, realizing that John A. was right about the lack of a written agreement. Not rattled, John A. simply changed the name of the motel to Fiddler's Inn South and raised the price even higher to $14.00 per night.

Joe Rodgers, an American construction company executive and the ambassador to France in the 1980s, came by and wanted to buy the property next to Fiddler's Inn South. Instead of selling it, John A. and Louis maintained ownership of the land and agreed to lease it to Rodgers, who subsequently built the Rodeway Inn.

Joe Rogers came to us wanting to build a hotel next door, but we didn't want to sell. We told him that we would lease it to him for a hundred fifty thousand a year. He thought that was fair enough, so I drew up the papers throwing in that we get 5 percent of his restaurant sales and a few other things. Then Joe Rogers became the ambassador to France and he held a lot of Republican meetings there, so we were doing really well with it.

Joe ended up building a few other hotels and sold the hotel he built on the land that we were leasing to him. He sold to Americana, which was owned by the Bass brothers out of the Fort Worth/Dallas area. Their daddy was Harry Richardson, one of the richest oilmen in America. When he died, he left his estate to these Bass boys. So, they wanted to sell the hotel, but they had a thirty-year lease on it. Several years of that lease had already been used, but after a couple of years, they came to me wanting to know if we wanted to buy it. They wanted seven million out of it to pay off what they owed, but I told them that it wasn't worth that much. I said, "We'll just let the lease run out on it and get it for nothing." They said, "You'll have to wait years on it," but I replied, "We're not in any hurry." Two weeks later they called and asked if we would give them three million for the hotel and we agreed. We took it over, remodeled it, and operated it for eight more years and then sold it and made a lot of money on it.

CHAPTER SEVENTEEN

Up Around the Bend

Y'all keep building, and I'll keep fiddlin'.
I'll see ya later!
—ROY ACUFF

o understand Music Valley today, one must learn the history and connect the key figures from the past that played important roles in her conception and development. This bend in the Cumberland River would be the location

Fiddler's Inn North construction on Music Valley Drive, circa 1971.

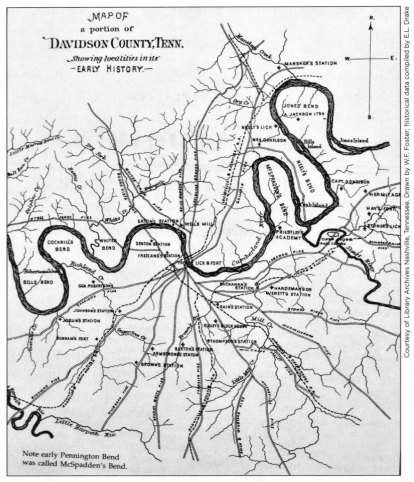

Davidson County early map of the Pennington Bend.

of the greatest amount of Middle Tennessee's transformation, which would determine the course of country music history for years to come. The efforts and dreams of those who had previously settled in the valley paved the way for visionaries such as John A. to recognize potential and to act without hesitation when opportunity knocked. John A. envisioned great opportunities in the area as did settlers several hundred years before him.

Graves Pennington was born around 1783 in Virginia and later traveled to Davidson County, Tennessee. It was here that he served in a militia defending the territory from Native American attacks. In return for his service, he was granted land in the bend. Graves Pennington was a wealthy businessman and plantation owner, and his land was inherited by his only son, John Pennington, who farmed the land and added land and resources to the estate.

Another important figure in early bend history was Thomas McSpadden Jr., whose property in the bend in 1809 totaled 239 acres. His father was Scotch-Irish and immigrated in the 1700s from Ireland. It was likely due to the large land holdings that the bend alternately took the Pennington and McSpadden names throughout the 1800s. It is unknown exactly when the bend took the official name of Pennington Bend that we refer to today.

Defining residents of the bend also included Jacob Ludwig Rudy, the son of Swiss immigrant Daniel Rudy and Mary (Zieger) Rudy, with his mom of German descent. As early as 1881, Daniel began making sausage for his family with a hand grinder brought from the motherland. He subsequently handed down the family trade to one of their ten children, Jacob Ludwig Rudy.

In 1911, Jacob married Katherine Clees, and they bore two sons, Frank and Dan Rudy. Katherine's ancestors, the Clees family, had immigrated from Luxembourg and originally settled in the Bells Bend area. They had several business endeavors, including a sawmill and a successful ferry service. Two of the Clees brothers, Joseph and Francis, moved to the Pennington Bend area and began another ferry service. When they died, they passed down the middle section of farmland, which is now Music Valley Drive, to Katherine Clees. Together, Jacob and Katherine Rudy built their home on the property, and in the 1920s and 1930s they passed the generations-old sausage recipe on to their sons, Frank and Dan Rudy.

Jacob Rudy died in 1936, leaving the farm to his wife Katherine, but Dan and Frank assumed the duties and expenses of the farm. During World War II, Frank and Dan increased the farming efforts, working approximately twelve hundred acres. Once the war had ended in 1945, the brothers drastically reduced the farming and incorporated their small, but growing sausage business. With the help of neighbors, a small plant was built, and they acquired a refrigerated truck for deliveries. By the late 1950s, Rudy's Farm was making and selling nearly five thousand pounds of sausage per month. In 1962 a modern plant meant to accommodate government inspection standards was built in the same Music Valley Drive location that the Hyatt Place and McDonald's now occupy. By 1970, the landscape of the bend was at the mercy of developers. The Rudy brothers had already sold their business to a company later acquired by the Sara Lee Corporation. Just over four hundred acres of Rudy farmland were sold to developers of the Opryland USA Theme Park, and Frank and Dan Rudy looked for opportunities to invest the millions they made off their business and farmland.[24]

The ground-breaking ceremony for the new Opryland USA Theme Park took place on June 30, 1970, on a portion of the Rudy's Farm on Pennington Bend. In 1972, the park opened its doors to visitors, offering world-class rides, water features, replica towns, and musical entertainment. After a visit to Disneyland in California, John A. envisioned the commerce that would accompany the construction of such a park and began developing his own ideas to capitalize on as much of the incoming business as he could.

I went to Disney in California to see my dad, who lived out there for a while. We went down to the park and sat on a bench looking around at all the motels and talked. I thought, "Boy, Walt Disney messed up." He built the park on four hundred and fifty acres, which is the same size as Opryland, because it was all that he could afford at the time. As soon as he built it, others came in and bought the land all around him where he couldn't expand. Walt Disney was way ahead of himself, but he didn't have the money to do it with. I was thinking, "Lord, I need to build a motel out there if they're fixing to build Opryland." When I came back to Nashville, I had that idea to build a motel in that area deep in my mind. We already owned a motel at I-40, and I had built a motel for my previous employers, Cartwright and Herman, a large construction company in Nashville, so I started my developing with a motel.

One day Frank Rudy came into my office. He and his brother Dan owned a successful sausage packing company. He said, "I'd liked to go in partnership with y'all on a motel and build it down on my farm." I called up Louis, who knew the Rudy family well, and we got in my car and drove down there to the land. We stepped off what we needed and put a broom stick down in each of the corners as markers. We discussed our terms of the partnership and ended up with half the land. Me, and brothers Pat, and Louis McRedmond, along with Frank and Dan Rudy, built the first motel, Fiddler's Inn North, and it did so well, we added to it. Then we added a campground, and The Nashville Palace.

We just kept growing down there until we bought twenty-five acres off of the Rudy family They made an unbelievable deal with us. We paid fifty thousand an acre for the land, but didn't put up a dime for it. We just paid for it out of the businesses. We became partners, but I built everything. We borrowed a million dollars from Commerce Union Bank and built the first two motel units. Then we had money left over, so we built a campground. It all worked out good for us. We rarely saw Dan or Frank Rudy, but we would mail out checks and they would come over once a year for a meeting. We made them a lot of money in our day.

While we were building our second motel out there, Roy Acuff dropped by to visit. He lived up on the hill across from the river and he could look down on our construction and watch us work. One day he drove over in his old Dodge and said, "Hey, Johnny! I've been watching you through the field glasses. What are y'all building here?"

I said, "A motel."

He said, "Boy, it needs one out here."

Ground-breaking ceremony for the wax museum, circa 1979. Left to right: Ken Shone, Pat McRedmond, Orba Maxey, Mrs. Harold Hensley, Bill Billingham, Louis McRedmond, Dan Rudy, and John A.

We sat down on a lumber pile talking about it, and I showed him the drawing and plans. It started to rain and Roy got up to leave. He said, "I just thought I'd drive on over here and see what you were building."

As he walked away, he said, "Y'all keep building, and I'll keep fiddlin'. I'll see ya later!"

I thought Fiddler's Inn would be a good name, so we named it after Roy Acuff, and we did good for many a year. When we built Fiddler's Inn North, I thought, "Well, we built the first two units and we'll probably only use them about eight months out of the year." So, I fixed it to where I could turn the water off to a unit, hook a compressor to it, and blow the water lines out. This way the units could sit all winter long without use. Luckily, I never had to blow the water lines out and let them sit all winter long, because the business was there year-round and we were doing well. That same time, Opryland was closing their theme park and hotel on Christmas Eve, and not reopening until the day after New Year's Day. I thought, "Damn, I am going to try and get that business," and we built another motel, raised the price, and went after it. I would see something else we could build around it like a campground, wax museum, car museum, and The Nashville Palace. We made it like a little city and we owned some of the first businesses in that valley.

CHAPTER EIGHTEEN

Music Valley Drive

We had four motels at one time, and for a boy
that never went to high school, my payroll was
nine hundred and sixty people.
—JOHN A. HOBBS

The strip of first businesses in the valley ran along a mile-long road that runs parallel to Briley Parkway and is right across the McGavock Pike entrance to the Opryland Hotel. With all the businesses being developed and with more people relocating to the area, the names in the area for things such as roads and streets had to be familiar to people so as to help with business and traffic flow. John A. knew this better than anyone and envisioned a name that would define the area for the rest of Nashville's history.

Music Valley Drive used to be named after Frank Rudy's father-in-law, Elzie Miller. We would get mail and everybody would call us to get a room and they'd say, "Where are you located?" I'd say, "E-L-Z-I-E Miller Road." "Elzie Miller? Where is that at?" I was out one day driving and I thought, "Man, we need to change the name of this street." I knew I would have to ask

125

Music Valley Drive pre-developmnent, circa 1970.

the Rudy family first because they were part owners of the hotel. I went over to their office in 1977 and said to them, "You may get mad at me, but I am telling you that I can't run a hotel down there with that name on it. It's too hard to pronounce and to spell."

Frank Rudy said, "That's my deceased father-in-law, and his widow is still living."

I said, "Well, I am going to try and get it changed."

He said, "I want you to, but don't tell anyone I said it."

I went to the councilman and I said, "Look, it's in a valley in the heart of music country, plus we've got Fiddler's Inn. Why don't we name it Music Valley Drive?" The councilman agreed, but wanted to know what the Rudy family had to say about it. I just told him that Frank didn't want his name mentioned, but wanted it changed, too. Not long after that,

Music Valley Drive pre-developmnents, from a different angle, circa 1973.

the signs went up with Music Valley Drive, and it was good for the whole city and everybody loved it.

Years ago, I let the bank trick me when interest on construction loans went to 20 percent at all banks. The bank came to us when we were building Fiddler's Inn claiming that they rated us "A-1" customers. They said, "Why don't you just keep it on a ninety-day note and pay what you want to once a year? Just pay the interest every month and in October and November, if you can pay a hundred dollars, five thousand, or twelve thousand, until you pay it off." I said, "Okay, we'll do it," never thinking about the interest going up.

Well, the interest rose to 20 percent on us and we were struggling without profits coming out. I said, "Louis, we made one bad mistake. If the interest ever gets down, we're going to lock it in." About three months later, the rates started dropping, and Louis said, "Do you want to freeze it?" I said, "Not yet. It's going to drop more." It did drop and got down to about 6 percent. We refinanced it and came out good. From then on, we never had any trouble with financing.

By 1987 nearly two and a half million people visited the Opryland Theme Park annually and more than seven hundred thousand stayed in nearby hotel rooms. John A. and his partners owned four hotels in the area by this time to capture a big chunk of the growing market.[25]

We were not in competition with the other motels because there is enough business for everybody out here. In 1985, we built the 308-room Music Valley Inn from scratch, which was operated as the Ramada Inn. It sat on eight acres owned by the Rudy family across from the Opryland Hotel on Music Valley Drive and McGavock Pike. I remember signing the initial development agreement in 1969. After completing

Pre-Ramada Hotel, Music Valley Drive, from opposite direction.

Post-development, Music Valley Drive aerial showing Ramada Hotel.

the paperwork, I joined some of the other developers for a walk around the property. When we went down there, we chased a horse around the field, and there were haystacks where the Ramada would be built years later.

We ran the Music Valley Inn for fourteen years and made good money with it. It was an upgrade from the other two hotels we owned. I had rooms up at I-40 cheaper, but then I raised Fiddler's Inn, and the Ramada. Then Louis and I bought the Rodeway Inn, which we already owned the ground under, and had them raise the price as well. With four different hotels, we could charge four different prices. When a couple would walk out of one location, you could tell them that you have another hotel down the way. I priced my rooms at Fiddler's Inn so that the ground floor was six dollars higher than the second floor because you could walk right into your room.

We were successful in building hotels, The Nashville Palace, car and wax museums, and more. All together we had twenty-eight businesses. We had four motels at one time, and for a boy that never went to high school, my payroll was nine hundred and sixty people. We had so many people working for us, that my computers couldn't print the paychecks all at once, so we paid every two weeks. Half of our staff we paid this week and the other half the following week. I had about fourteen people working in my office and my sister, Joann, was running everything for us.

Now, the boys modernized our business, and they cut out a lot of that waste. They have three girls working in the office, and they are going about it the right way. Your office can kill you with overhead costs. My son, Ronnie Hobbs, was running all the motels, and he did an outstanding a job, so we did really well. Honestly, without Ronnie's help, we couldn't have done any of it. I was so proud that all my boys helped in the businesses. Joe helped to build and Mike helped us a lot in the beginning. Other big investors made a fortune in Nashville, but I thought they were the dumbest people I had ever dealt with. I would watch other hotel managers and do exactly the opposite and I made money. I thought, "Well, that was stupid, but it's good because I am making money off what he's doing wrong."

Running motels is not all gravy; you have to watch what's going on. One woman checked in one time and she cooked in the bathtub. She plugged a cooktop in and could've electrocuted herself, but it got real hot and melted through the tub. Of course, she didn't tell us. She threw dirty towels in it and left town.

One morning I was up at Fiddler's Inn South and Louis came by, so we were talking out in the parking lot. Suddenly, a car wheeled around real fast and the driver somehow knew what room to go into. He kicked the room door down and his wife was in there with another man, but this guy with her had climbed into the bathtub and pulled the curtain across so that the husband couldn't see him. Her husband grabbed her by the arm and brought her out of the room. He put her in the car and looked over at us. He said, "Y'all own this hotel?"

I said, "Yes."

"I'll pay for the damages, but is it okay if I leave her car here and pick it up tomorrow?"

I said, "Leave it as long as you want to," and he left. So, that old boy come out of there trying to light a cigarette. I said, "You better get in that car and get out of here. He knows who you are already because he knew what room you were in." He left out of there really quick. I said, "Boy, just keep going."

I went down there one day and another guy had kicked the door in. He was mad that his wife had locked him out.

He started pushing her around, so, I went out to the car and got a pistol. I put the gun in my back pocket and went on in the room.

I said, "Cut it out right now!"

He said, "This is my wife!"

I said, "I don't care who it is, you're not going to beat on her. You get out of here or I am going to have you taken out of here! Whichever way you want to go."

I turned to the woman and said, "You get your clothes on and you get out of here, too. I am going to stand outside the door until you leave."

They both came out still arguing. I said, "Well, you're not leaving yet. You owe us for the door you kicked in."

He said, "What would that cost us?"

I said, "A hundred bucks!" He paid it, but we had stuff like that all the time.

Louis McRedmond was worth twenty-five million, but he always worked and never went anywhere. He always wanted to go to Alaska, but never would go. One day he was in my office and said, "One of these days, I am going to Alaska." As soon as he left, I called a travel company and purchased four tickets to Alaska.

I called him up and I said, "Get ready! We're leaving next Monday for Alaska."

He said, "You've already purchased the tickets?"

I said, "Yeah, so tell your wife to get ready."

We went to Alaska and then the World Series was on, and he'd never been to a Major League Baseball game. They were playing in Los Angeles, so I called my friend and manager of the Dodgers, Tommy Lasorda, and asked for ten tickets. We got out there, and Louis had the best time of his life. We went to the World Series and toured the city.

That night, we were going out to Bob Smith's house, he's vice president of the Dodgers, to have a little party. Now, I don't drive when I am drinking. So, while we were at the ballpark, I said to my bookkeeper, "Bill, here's the keys to the van, I am going to let you drive." I had rented a fifteen-passenger van for everyone, and I handed over the keys. My bookkeeper didn't drink, but I didn't realize he was such a bad driver.

Well, we came out of there and he liked to have had a wreck. He didn't know how to drive on the freeway. I thought, "He's going to get us killed!" We headed out to Bob's house and Bill is all mixed up. I said, "We have to turn in a block up here, so get in the left lane." He gets screwed up and misses it, but finally we get there. Louis and I had two or three more drinks at the party. As we left, Louis patted me on the arm and said, "Look Johnny, I'd rather ride with you drunk than with Bill sober."

CHAPTER NINETEEN

The Nashville Palace

It was an interesting, interesting place for many years.
It wasn't anything to see stars in there. I could go on
for a hundred years and not tell you all the things
that went on in there.

—JOHN A. HOBBS

John A. offered his boys some advice, saying,

"Boys you can't get rich overnight; it doesn't happen. Very few people can make a hundred million dollars really quick. If you're making good money, you're making two or three hundred thousand a year. You better stick with that business until it goes down, but try to open a side business and be ready for it."

I never was a big gambler to go out and really run a high risk, but if I could make three hundred thousand dollars a year, that's what I'd do.

Louis McRedmond and John A. worked various partnerships with the Rudy family and accumulated a large amount of land from the Rudy farm as a result. Whatever John A. said he wanted to do in business, Louis supported him, and they did well as a result. Together Louis and John A. built a small city complete with car museums, featuring antique and classic cars owned by the stars, a wax museum, Marty Robbins Museum, Boxcar Willie Railroad Museum, Music Valley Village Shopping Center, and the Fiddler's Inn Campground. They developed real estate occupied by Ernest Tubb's Western Wear, a Country and Western Sightseeing Company, Loretta Lynn Western Wear, a Quik Pix one-hour photo shop, and the Willie Nelson Museum. Add to that, several liquor stores, two drive-up markets, a go-kart track, miniature golf course, six tobacco stores, and a gas station. The Hobbs family smartly placed each of the businesses under different corporations and flourished. Some of the businesses the Rudy family went in on; others, they simply couldn't afford to. In 1993, John A.'s construction firm built Factory Stores of America and in the following year, the Music Valley Village shopping center went in. Music Valley Village contained more than twenty-five retail businesses including western shops, a record store, gift boutiques, and restaurants. Also located in the village was the Stardust Theater featuring Boots Randolph and Danny Davis, and the Texas Troubadour Theater, which aired the world-famous *Midnite Jamboree* every Saturday night.

Of all the businesses created in Music Valley, The Nashville Palace at 2400 Music Valley Drive was by far the most iconic and the biggest that would gain John A. worldwide notoriety. In 1977 John A. built the legendary honkytonk at a cost of about four hundred fifty thousand dollars with partners Pat and Louis McRedmond. Frank and Dan Rudy were partners in a separate corporation that owned and leased the land that The Palace was built on. John A. came up with the name for his Palace based on

Fan Fair Party at The Palace, circa 1983. Left to right: Johnson Sisters, John A., and Loretta Lynn.

The Palace Theater in Hollywood, California. There were only two places in all of Nashville to go out to, Buddy Killen's Stock-Yard, located downtown or The Nashville Palace. Millions of tourists streamed into the area for the theme park, the Grand Ole Opry, and the other local attractions, and hundreds of thousands stayed in the hotel rooms and campgrounds nearby. The area desperately needed a restaurant and entertainment venue to accommodate the nightlife, and John A. envisioned it and built it. The Nashville Palace both attracted and created some of the biggest stars in country music.

Every big star in Nashville showed up on opening night, and we had between seven and eight hundred people come and it only seated four hundred and fifty. People were standing everywhere, and there were long lines out front to get in. You wouldn't believe it; Ralph Emery, Johnny Rodriguez, Jim Ed Brown, Chet Atkins, the Tennessee governor, the mayor of Nashville, the county sheriff, and everybody was there that night. I had two stages going, one on each side of the venue. One side seated about a hundred fifty people, and the other side seated roughly up to three hundred. It had a main dining room where you could eat and enjoy the show. I had two stages running at first, but found out really quick, it was too complicated, so I took one stage out.

Back in the old days, let's go back to the 1960s and 1970s, there were a lot of old stars at the Opry. They were all good people. You know I never treated them like stars, because they were friends. We stayed friends until each one of them died. Roy Acuff was a good man and helped a lot of people. Boxcar Willie was a fine gentleman, too. Their word was good and you never had to worry about any contracts. I booked everybody, Jim Ed Brown, Boxcar Willie, Johnny Russell, Del Reeves, Jimmy Dickens, Jeannie Seely, and all the old-timers. I found out that they were the nicest people on earth. They never considered themselves big stars and they were down-to-earth. We didn't consider it as working for us, we all worked together.

The Palace was nothing when it started, but we decided to build a nightclub because there wasn't a whole lot going on in the valley. At that time, there were four campgrounds that could accommodate two thousand campers, and each camper had three or four people in it. We needed something to take care of people at night, so we built the club. When we were building it, we didn't know what we were going to

The site of Jerry Reed's Palace, circa 1976. Left to right: Bill Billingham, John A., Jerry Reed, Louis McRedmond, and Mike Walsh

name it. Initially, I worked a deal with Marty Robbins and asked him if we could put his name on it for one year. He signed the contract and agreed to it, but Opryland wasn't very happy. They said he was too big of a name and didn't want to compete with him across the street. Marty Robbins called me up one day and said, "Johnny, I want to buy back my contract because Opryland is mad that I am over here." I said, "I'll tear it up and mail it to you. Don't worry about it, you don't have to pay me anything, we'll get someone else."

About that time, Jerry Reed's manager came by and asked us what we were building, and I ended up making a deal with Jerry Reed. Jerry was a country singer, guitar player, songwriter, and actor. The deal was signed right before he made *Smokey and the Bandit* with Burt Reynolds. The contract was for ten thousand dollars for one year, and during that year Jerry had to come in to the club at least thirty times. Turns out that Jerry was well worth the money because he came out there every night and brought a lot of stars with him. So, our first year we called it Jerry Reed's Palace.

When I signed Jerry Reed for a year, we put signs out there in front, parking only for Jerry Reed's Palace. You know people would steal everything with his name on it. I couldn't leave anything out there with his name on it because they would take it. I went in a club downtown one night and I saw one of my signs in there that they took off my lot. It was funny, but we made ashtrays because back then everybody smoked, except me. I never smoked a day in my life, but we had ashtrays with his name and a nice logo. It wasn't really worth a lot of money to us, but they stole every one of them. I just quit using his name for advertisement, except for in the paper and other places.

Jerry Reed was a good fella, but after he made it big with Burt Reynolds and Sally Field in *Smokey and the Bandit*, he came in one day and said, "Johnny, I've got to have fifty thousand per year now to use my name." I said, "Jerry, then I have to rub your name off, because I am not going to pay fifty thousand for it. Your name is probably worth it, but we just can't pay that kind of money for a name." So, we just called it The Palace and later we changed it to The Nashville Palace.

After his divorce from Mary, John A. stayed single and took up residence on the top floor at the Fiddler's Inn North. He had a suite that included a large outdoor patio with a porch swing looking out toward the club, just a short stroll away. You can still drive by the hotel today and see the patio and suite he occupied above the lobby. As you pull up out front, you can almost hear the laughter and storytelling that must have poured out of those walls. Imagine all the fun times and legendary characters that John A. played host to in that space. Many of the stars loved to stop by and see him, eat white beans and cornbread, and visit. These were the happiest times of John A.'s life, and he can't help but smile when he tells the stories.

I stayed single for five years living out at the Fiddler's Inn, in a suite on the second floor. I had a patio with a swing, and all the Opry stars used to stop and see me. On Saturday mornings, they would do a show at the Opry house, then come over about eleven o'clock. The ones that drank would drink and Little Jimmy Dickens, who we called "Tater," loved to have a good time. Little Jimmy Dickens, Johnny Russell, Del Reeves, and Jim Ed Brown. Jim Ed was one of my best friends and he would always come by and see me after the Opry show and we would talk. When it snowed, I used to give them all a room at the motel so they didn't have to drive. Grant Turner was an announcer over there and couldn't drive all the way down to Murray Lane in Brentwood, so I'd say, "Just come on over and I'll give you a room." One time, Little Jimmy Dickens was standing in the lobby with snow all over him. It was snowing hard with about ten inches on the ground and Jimmy needed two rooms. I told the girl at the front desk to give him the keys to two rooms, but only charge him for the one. He was glad to have the two rooms because he had some kin folks with him that night.

Del Reeves used to come by and knock on my door at three o-clock in the morning and say, "I am not driving all the way back down to my home, I am going to sleep on your couch." He told me he was hungry, so, I got some white beans out and heated them up with cornbread. I chopped up white onion and we ate white beans and cornbread and told stories about things that had happened.

Del was a lot of fun to be around, and we just had a good time together. These were probably some of the happiest times of my life. It snowed one night and I woke up freezing. I jumped up out of bed and the hotel door was wide open with it snowing outside. I didn't see Del and come to find out, he had left to go downstairs to meet a friend.

He came back up after a while and said, "Man alive, I want to tell you, I didn't know it was so cold out there! Why did you shut the door on me?"

I said, "Because you were freezing me! Don't leave the door open anymore."

In the morning, he was sawing logs, but had to be in Indianapolis at one-thirty and do a show on Sunday. I said, "How are you going to get there? The roads are slick."

He said, "My bus is going to pick me up." He left out of there on that bus and went on up and did the show, came back the next night and stayed again with me. Unfortunately, Del died quite a few years ago from emphysema.

Jack Greene used to come up there, and we would just sit and talk all night long. I heard good stories from all of them about true things that had happened to them in their lives. Jack Greene used to work for Ernest Tubb, and when he made "Statue of a Fool," it became a hit, and he was moving up. Ernest Tubb fired him because Jack wouldn't quit and Ernest wanted him to go on his own, because he knew he could do it. Jack did go on his own, scared to death, but he did well.

A lot of the stars used to come around all the time in The Palace. Del Reeves was there all the time. Every time Johnny Russell came into town, he was there. I remember one night; Mel Tillis just walked in and went up right on stage and started singing. A lot of them would do that, just walk in and get up on stage. Johnny Russell weighed about three hundred pounds and he would get up on stage and say, "Can y'all see me?"

Johnny Russell used to come in The Nashville Palace, and he ordered blackberry cobbler on a big platter. God, it'd be a big bowlful, and he'd eat it every night out there. He loved that blackberry cobbler and the catfish, too.

One night, he came to me and said, "John, I need a room. Me and my wife separated."

She had thrown him out and it was raining, so I gave him a suite where he would be comfortable at the Ramada. He said, "Johnny, she's thrown my clothes out in the rain where all of the neighbors will see them, but I can't go out and pick them up."

So, I sent my laundry truck with two men out there to pick them up for him. I got two racks out of one of my clothing store, and set them up over paper where his clothes could drip dry overnight.

A night at The Nashville Palace, circa 1980.

A lot of stars came in to The Palace on a regular basis and they all played music there. John A. used to book them on Monday nights and call it, "Opry Night." He would have them lined up in early spring for the next year. Jim Ed Brown was a good friend of John A.'s and would frequently stop by and say hello. Although John A. never officially hired him, Roy Acuff would go on stage all of the time. It was a hot bed of entertainment and artists made it a highlight in their tour-packed schedules to perform there. Numerous stars and artists graced The Palace stage during the thirty-year run. Big names like Brad Paisley, Garth Brooks, Tammy Wynette, Patty Loveless, Ernest Tubb, Jimmy Dickens, Jerry Reed, Marty Robbins, Johnny Cash, Willie Nelson, Del Reeves, Johnny Russell, Boxcar Willie, Waylon Jennings, George Jones, Mel Tillis, Jack Greene, Porter Wagoner, and many, many more. Dottie West was on the scheduled to sing, but died before she had the chance. Webb Pierce was such a regular that he had his own cooler in the back of the bar.

> So many of the stars liked to come out here, and sometimes I would have eight or ten stars and they would all sit around and talk.

It was truly a place to gaze at the stars and they advertised as such. On any given night, you never knew what star would be in there. The memorabilia on the walls was a who's who of Nashville and of country music. Even more incredible was the fact that John A. graciously provided a venue for aspiring artists to gain experience and exposure. Alan Jackson, Ricky Van Shelton, Randy Travis, and Lorrie Morgan were just a few that credit The Palace and John A. for their successful country music career starts.

Boxcar Willie was one of my closest friends. One night Boxcar came in and saw Anna Mae Johnson singing onstage. She was in her late sixties and had a wholesome and grand-motherly presence. He said, "My God, Johnny, where'd you find her?" He suggested that we promote her as the "Singing Grandma." It wasn't long before she became the tradition at The Nashville Palace. When she died, she had it written in her will that she wanted the funeral procession to make a stop by The Nashville Palace on the way to the airport. This was so all her dear friends could say one last good-bye. The funeral director stopped the hearse in front of The Palace and everyone came out to pay their respects.

John A. was bestowed the wreath that lay on her casket, and it hung in her memory over the cash register at The Nashville Palace for years.

CHAPTER TWENTY

Providing the Exposure

We never made a star, but we gave the artist
an opportunity for exposure. A singer has to do a lot of work
in smoke-filled bars to be a good singer.
—JOHN A. HOBBS

Alan Jackson credits his career start to The Nashville Palace and the exposure that John A. was willing to provide at his club. At the time, Alan worked in the mailroom at the Opry across the road. He used to come into The Palace every night and ask John A. if he could get up and sing. It wasn't long after this that Alan became the first country artist signed to Arista Records, and his long and successful career in music was off and running.

> Alan Jackson used to come in every night about nine-thirty and ask, "Can you let me sing up on the stage?"
>
> I would say, "Well, yeah, they'll work you in."
>
> He'd say, "I am so tired. I am going out to sleep in my van. Will you come out and wake me up when it's time?"
>
> We sent someone out to wake him up when the time came to get up on stage and sing.

Alan Jackson, Tommy Lasorda, and John A., circa 1999.

By the late nineties, Alan Jackson was a country music superstar with more than seventy awards, twenty-two number-one hits, twenty-five million records sold, and membership in the Grand Ole Opry. When his album, *Under the Influence*, was released in October 1999, he did a live broadcast from The Palace for the premiere. When the disc jockey asked Alan why he chose The Palace to have the premiere, he said it was because The Nashville Palace is where he got his start. He reminisced with the audience and his worldwide listeners about his first time on stage at The Palace. The Nashville Palace house band was the Steve Hill Band, and they backed Alan up while he sang songs like John Conlee's, "Rose Colored Glasses."

"This place will always hold that memory for me," Alan said.

> Alan Jackson could write a song quicker than anyone I ever knew. You know he could write a song overnight, and he was just a damn good songwriter and a good performer, too. Polite and nice. You wouldn't believe this, but today

when I see him, he says, "Mr. Hobbs, how are you?" He still
calls me Mr. Hobbs, and I said, "Why don't you call me John?"
He never would do it, but he was a damn good boy and is a
damn good man.

Other notables crediting The Nashville Palace for their early
career success include Lorrie Morgan. Her father was the country
music singer, George Morgan, best known for a hit called "Candy
Kisses." George had been a member of the Grand Ole Opry since
1948 and was inducted into the Country Music Hall of Fame.
He died in 1975 from a heart attack after undergoing open heart
surgery, but Lorrie carried on her father's legacy.[26] When she first
came to The Palace, she wasn't old enough to sit at the bar. John A.

Keith Whitley, Lorrie Morgan and friend, and John A.

gave her on one of her first singing jobs, besides the Opry, to help her out after her father died. Lorrie said that The Nashville Palace gave her the opportunity to learn how to work with a crowd, helped prepare her to become an entertainer, and helped her to mature as a performer working with a professional band. She said, it also helped her by knowing that someone important might be in the audience.

In the early eighties, Randy Traywick along with his music manager Elizabeth "Lib" Hatcher dropped by The Palace looking for work and a place where Randy could perform. Randy was hired primarily as a dishwasher and cook, but he filled in wherever he was needed. Lib became the manager and cook at the club and did a solid job of it for years. She kept good food in the house and was a phenomenal cook as well. She was always pestering John A. to stock her with certain foods and one time it backfired on her.

> One time I remember, Lib Hatcher kept pestering me to get fresh corn. I hadn't had time to get to the market and get it, and I think she hit me wrong asking about it one Sunday morning. I took a pickup truck to the market and loaded it full of fresh corn, right out of the field. I brought it back to The Palace, and Randy was washing dishes. I knocked on the door and they opened the door and I said, "Lib, I got a little corn out here for you." I had a whole truckload!
>
> She said, "Oh, my God! Randy! Randy! Go out there and get that corn, and we're gonna shuck it right now!" He looked over at me and said, "Today was my day off." I felt sorry for him, but she had him in there shucking that corn until late that night. When Randy came back to The Palace to sing, he was a big star with a big hit, I had a bushel of corn sent up to the stage with a knife. He leaned back and laughed.

Like many stars and people in Nashville, John A. helped Randy Travis when he was down and out and didn't have any money. Randy was treated like family and John A. gave him several suits of clothes, belts and buckles, boots, and shirts. Randy Travis loved to have the opportunity to get out of the kitchen, borrow one of the western-wear sport coats, and get up on stage to sing a couple of songs or do a show for the crowd. John A. still has a picture hanging in his restaurant of Randy Travis, when he was the dishwasher at The Palace for five years, before making it big. Travis:

> "The early days at The Nashville Palace were the turning point in my career, no doubt. John A. Hobbs owned The Palace. One of my first few days on the job, I spent the whole day taking apart and cleaning the greasy exhaust vent over the stove. I don't think it was the popular thing to do, but when John A. found out, he gave me a raise and has treated me like family ever since. I love the man. At The Palace, I cooked, cleaned, bussed tables, was the handyman, and sang. I slept a few hours a day. I had the chance to record *Randy Ray Live* while there. One night Martha Sharp with Warner Bros. A&R came in to hear me. I guess I had what she was looking for. Nothing was quite the same after that. I love that lady to this day. I'll never forget The Palace or Mr. Hobbs. It was a great place to see all kinds of talent and have an excellent meal."

John A. was instrumental in creating Randy's much-needed second album, *Randy Ray, Live at The Nashville Palace*, and paved the way for his success by providing exposure. Every aspiring artist craves exposure, and it would be nightly exposure on the coveted Palace stage, alongside the biggest names in country music, that would launch Randy's career. Every major record label in town had turned him down for being "too country," but Lib kept promoting him anyway. Tom Powell, longtime senior editor of *Amusement Business*, recalls how persistent Lib was when it came to promotion.

> "Lib Hatcher was the manager of The Palace, and every time I would get a picture of Del Reeves or Porter Wagoner, or somebody, Lib would make sure that Randy got in the picture. So, his picture went up in *Amusement Business* a lot of times. So much so that Ronnie Robbins, Marty Robbins's son, once said to me, "How can I get my picture in *Amusement Business* as much as Randy Travis?" I said, "Well, get Lib Hatcher as your manager."

Lib Hatcher pushed to get Randy interviews and on television shows, the Opry, and *The Nashville Now Show* with Ralph Emery. John A. said that Ralph Emery is one of the nicest men he has ever known. Ralph would always give plugs for The Nashville Palace on the show, and John A. returned the favor by delivering catfish down there for him to be able to eat before the show. Randy was usually the delivery man of that gifted food, and Ralph promised to get Randy on his show. Ralph Emery was true to that promise, and Randy Travis performed on *The Nashville Now Show* several times. Randy was televised in 1983 at The Palace singing, "I Told You So" in front of a live audience and appeared on the television show, *You Can Be a Star*, which was an amateur talent show hosted by Jim Ed Brown, Bobby Randall, and Lisa Foster.

> Lib Hatcher managed Randy, and she really wanted him to get on the Opry. So, Little Jimmy said, "Come over Saturday night and I'll give you one of my spots." It was Little Jimmy Dickens, who gave Randy his first time on the Grand Ole Opry and his first new guitar. Ralph Emery stayed true to

his word and put Randy on his show and that really helped Randy with his start. He wanted his first major record, so we bought the record and gave it to him as a bonus.

With showmanship in mind, Randy later changed his name to Randy Ray and finally, with his Warner Brothers record deal, he changed to his well-known stage name of Randy Travis. Country music singer Neal McCoy remembers his experiences at The Nashville Palace and with his friend Randy Travis, who was known as Randy Ray at the time.

McCoy: The first time I met Randy Travis, it was very brief, but then I would run into him throughout the years of us playing together or working together. The first time I met him, was in 1982 or 1983, at one of these Nashville Palace audition things. The winners of the contest got to go to Nashville and perform on the Grand Ole Opry. It was pretty cool, and it had two winners. I won for the state of Texas and a little girl named Martina McBride won for the state of Kansas. I

John A. and Randy Travis

didn't know her, but we met there at the contest. The joke that Martina and I still tell is that neither one of us finished in the top ten, but for the life of us, we can't remember who won. We just remember that we didn't.

After the competition, a bunch of us contestants migrated over to The Nashville Palace. I believe at the time he was still Randy Ray, and he was performing there. I don't know if he was still washing dishes in the early eighties, he may have been just performing on the side. I think Randy was supposed to be working that night, and a bunch of us hoodlums, you know, wannabes in our early twenties, came in to The Palace. We certainly didn't take over, but we all gathered around the piano and just started singing in the round. Randy was a little upset about it. I think he thought, "First of all, who are these young kids, what dues have they paid? They won a contest and here they are taking over some of my time." I understood it. I could see that he probably wasn't very happy about it. I told him about that over the years. That was my first experience with The Nashville Palace. Man, we had heard about it, so as little ole contestants, we thought, "Oh, my gosh, The Nashville Palace!" It was a huge deal for us because I remember when I got back to Longview, Texas, I was saying that I got to sing at The Nashville Palace and the Grand Ole Opry. It was like, "I'll just die now." I started at the top and worked my way slowly down.

Randy and I were friends through the music business; we'd run into each other and we had mutual respect for each other. I obviously had more respect for him because he was so huge; by the time I had any hits under my belt in the early nineties, he was already in five or six years of big hits. Other than The Palace, there wasn't many places to go watch live talent. They had the market cornered because people would leave from the Opryland Hotel and they'd leave the Opry and they could just go across the street to catch some good live talent and delicious food, and a great hangout. It gives them an opportunity to be noticed because all the people that used to go in The Palace, from producers to writers to singers to just everybody in the business, would migrate over that direction. So, you never knew who was in the house.

John A. always had good advice for those in business, and he had a great eye and ear for musical talent that he would pass on to the many young singers that would knock on his door wanting to be big stars.

I tell people, they may have started at The Nashville Palace, but we couldn't make them a star. They had to have a lot of talent when they walked in. We would give them a break and give them the exposure by allowing them onstage. I tell young people that come to me now, "You don't become a singer overnight, it takes a long time." You don't become a bricklayer overnight either. First, if you're building houses, you have to mix mortar, and you have to know what you're doing. If you are going to be a star, you can't just go onstage. There's more to it than just singing. It's the way you present yourself on the stage.

Dianne Sherrill is one of the best I've ever seen with stage presence. I've helped a lot of people in a lot of ways with their careers. I could see what they were doing on the stage and I would tell them what they were doing wrong. I figured I am an average fan when I am sitting out there in the audience. Randy Travis never would smile. Randy was a good kid, but I used to say, "Randy, smile! You never smile, you look awful sad and you should always smile while you're onstage." I know Randy Travis has said that he's seldom opened a show without asking if anyone in the audience remembers seeing him at The Nashville Palace. He says he always gets a loud holler, or some applause, when he did that. To me that shows how much he appreciates what The Palace was able to do for him.

Randy married his manager, Lib Hatcher, in the early nineties after years of concealing their romance. He continued his upward movement in the music industry with hits like "Forever and Ever Amen," "Diggin' Up Bones," and "I Told You So." He also became an actor playing parts in several movies and in a popular television series. In 2010 Randy and Lib were divorced and in 2013, Randy suffered a massive stroke, which proved to be a huge setback. In 2015 he married Mary Davis, and with rehabilitation has regained his ability to walk with the assistance of a cane and even sang "Amazing Grace" at his induction into the Country Music Hall of Fame in October 2016.[27] It was an event attended by the very proud and longtime supporter of Randy, Mr. John A. Hobbs.

By creating The Nashville Palace, John A. forever changed the course of country music history. It truly was the best place to see and be seen, and he was the conduit of it all. There were untold numbers of famous stars—past, present, and future—who congregated at The Nashville Palace, generating nothing less than an atmosphere of legendary proportions.

CHAPTER TWENTY-ONE

Young Ricky Van Shelton

*The good part is that a lot of friends helped me all the way
through my life, and I helped people. I hate to hear somebody say,
'I made it all on my own.' There's no man who can make it on his
own, and be an island by himself. I don't give a damn who he is,
he's got to have help from somebody, somewhere. That's the reason
I helped a lot of stars get their start.*
—JOHN A. HOBBS

Ricky Van Shelton is a very successful country music
singer who also has a connection with The Nashville
Palace and John A. As a boy, Ricky Van loved to sing
and would do so every chance he had. That included singing
gospel music at his church. As a teenager, he discovered his love
for country music and performed at fish fries and other events
with his brother and friends. In the early eighties, Ricky Van
moved to Nashville with his wife-to-be, Bettye Witt, and rented
a place just a few miles from The Nashville Palace. Ricky Van
would go down to The Nashville Palace each night, after Bettye
went to bed, to make connections and to sing, just hoping that
the right person would hear him.

Ricky Van: We left the twenty-sixth of December in 1984 and headed to Nashville because Bettye believed in my music and I did, too. That's where I wanted to be, and I wanted to try and make it in the music world, so we headed out there. The plan was for me not to work. I would stay home and take care of the house, inside and out. I'd wash dishes, vacuum and do all that stuff and take care of the yard, too, and Bettye would make the money. Then, at night time, after she got home and we ate supper, she would go to bed, and I would go to The Nashville Palace and try to meet people and get up and sing. I had a definite plan. I found out really quick the house band were all professionals, a lot of professional players stopped in there, and a lot of the Opry stars would come over and eat between shows. So, I knew I found the right spot to get discovered.

Johnny Russell, circa 1979.

Ricky Van was young and eager to learn how to be successful in the music industry and wisely sought the advice of country music veteran Johnny Russell.

> "I was there for a purpose, you know. I was asking everybody, who's this guy right there, can he help me? I had a plan. I didn't go down there to just party at all. I was down there to make a difference in my life. My wife, Bettye, made that possible. So many people heard me sing down there, and there were people coming in to hear me sing. Of course, Randy Travis was working there, too, and he and I became buddies, and we still are buddies. I never will forget those days."

John A. remembers young Ricky Van at The Palace and always thought the world of him.

> You know, we helped a lot of stars and a lot of them came by The Palace. You know who had the best voice I ever listened to at The Palace, was Ricky Van Shelton. Ricky Van had a southern accent from Virginia. He was good, he smiled, and I loved to hear him sing a song. He had something in his voice that you really listened to.
>
> He came in one time when I was hanging out with Johnny Russell. The young singer told us that he wanted to be a star and asked for advice, which we gladly gave. Just a few months later he had a big hit on the radio, and Johnny Russell turned to me and asked, "What did I tell Ricky Van to do? Whatever it was, I need to do that." When Ricky Van made it big, he used to come into The Palace and bring his band to do a show for us for free.

The Nashville Palace quickly became one of Ricky Van's favorite spots to perform. Steve Hill, band leader for The Palace, always made him feel welcome on stage to sing with them.

Ricky Van conctinues: I had more fun and was more thrilled singing there at The Nashville Palace than any show I did professionally. I was young, I was eager, and I was just beaming inside. I could hardly sing sometimes for grinning. I was in hog heaven.

One night, after I got to know the band, with Steve Hill, the bass player for the house band, he said, 'Let me introduce you to Mr. Hobbs, he owns this place.' So, he carried me over there to Mr. Hobbs and introduced me. Mr. Hobbs immediately took to me and said, in that old gravelly voice he's got, "Man, I love your voice, where are you from?"

He started asking me all of these questions. He was genuinely interested and that made me feel so good. Then he said, "Let me buy you a beer."

I said, 'I appreciate it, but I don't like to drink when I sing.'

He said, 'That is really, really good!' I made a major brownie point with him right there, but I wasn't trying to, I was just being truthful with him.

Young Ricky Van Shelton performing at The Nashville Palace, circa 1985.

"John A. has a heart of gold and is always tuned in to a person's situation, offering assistance without solicitation.

"I didn't have any money because Bettye was making the money for both of us, and we were living from week to week. So, I might have five dollars a night to tip the waitresses with. I couldn't buy a beer, which I didn't want a beer because I don't like to drink when I play music anyway. I didn't want to be a bum, so I would just order a glass of water, and I'd give the waitress the tip.

"Mr. Hobbs, would always call me over to him or come over and start talking. Always telling me what a good job I did. He asked me, 'You need any money, son?'

I said, 'No sir, I am good.'

He said, 'If you ever need anything, you just let me know.' He would say, 'Ricky Van, you hungry?' I'd say, 'No, sir, I am not hungry.' He'd tell one of the waitresses that came by, 'Bring this boy something to eat.' He was just so good to me and he didn't have to be. I was nobody, but that's the way he is. He was so successful, but he didn't care who you were. He was real and just won my heart over. I am so thankful that Mr. Hobbs was there to talk to me. He gave me confidence when I was down there trying to make it. It's not that you want a pat on the back, nobody wants a false pat on the back. However, when you find somebody of his caliber, that's genuinely interested in you as a person, and says you did a great job, you know he means it. I never will forget him.

Jerry Thompson, a well-known columnist for *The Tennessean*, heard a cassette demo of Ricky Van's voice and instantly realized the incredible talent in him. They met one day and really hit it off and as a result, Jerry decided to do everything in his power to help him succeed.

"Bettye was personnel manager working with Jerry's wife, Linda. They became best friends, and I was making all these little cassette tapes in our basement of my original songs. Bettye gave one to Linda, and she gave it to Jerry, because Jerry loved country music. Jerry knew everybody in the world. He knew Rick Blackburn, president of CBS. He knew all those people, so he and I became friends and he heard my music. He carried me to CBS one day and they set up a showcase for me. I got a record deal out of it, and that's how the whole thing started."

The very same year, with Jerry Thompson serving as his manager, Ricky Van recorded his debut album called, *Wild-Eyed Dream*. The title song from the album did well. A second song, "Crime of Passion," pulled from this same album, made an even bigger splash on the country music charts, reaching the top ten. It just kept getting better, and Ricky Van's career grew stronger with each platinum record and every major award he could win including Top New Male Vocalist in 1988 at the ACM awards show and Male Vocalist of the Year at the CMA awards show in 1989. In 1987, Ricky Van had become a member of the Grand Ole Opry, something that he had dreamed of his entire life.[28]

"I remember being so overwhelmed the night I was inducted into the Opry. I had been listening to the Opry all my life and never dreamed I would ever be a member. Jack Greene and Roy Acuff introduced me as their newest member and asked me to sing "Somebody Lied." I received a standing ovation and was asked to do an encore. At that point, I was so emotionally overwhelmed, I forgot the words. It was truly one of the most memorable events in my life."

John A. Hobbs served on the board of the Academy of Country Music at the pinnacle of Ricky Van's career and remembers traveling with him and Bettye out to Los Angeles for the awards show.

> Ricky Van was afraid to fly, and we were all going to the awards show together, but we were going to fly out there. We all arrive at the airport, and Ricky Van tells me that he has to have a drink before he can get on the plane. We went over and had a drink before boarding. We were flying out there in first class and there were a lot of stars sitting up there with us. Alan Jackson was there with his wife, and he was wearing a white sport coat. Well, me and Ricky Van continued drinking while standing up in the front cabin and he accidentally spilled his drink right on Alan. Alan didn't get mad or anything, but I would have. I got tickled and the stewardess came over and said, "Let me tell you something. You two are having a big time, but you both either have to sit down in your seats or go to the back of the plane." Ricky Van said, "Hmm, okay! Let's go to the back of the plane."
>
> We went to the back of the plane and we just had a big time. When we landed, I rented a big fifteen-passenger van to carry all of us to the hotel. So, we throw all our luggage in there and head out to the Universal Hilton Hotel. We're having a big time along the way and there was a man on the corner selling peanuts. I pulled the van over and we bought about five bags each of roasted peanuts and we're dropping them on the ground. Next, we stopped at the beer gardens and finally go on out to the hotel. We had a lot of fun getting there.

Ricky Van wouldn't stay in a hotel unless his room was located below the fourth floor, not because he was afraid of heights, but because he had already experienced one West Coast earthquake. His biggest fear was his fear of flying, which was a real prob-lem with booking long-distance dates. But, he faced that fear and sought out flight lessons in Lebanon, Tennessee, with his wife Bettye. He earned his pilot's license and bought a small, twin-en-gine plane to commute to shows.

> Ricky Van: I was scared to fly back then in the early days, but I became a pilot later. I turned down a whole lot of shows, because I wouldn't fly. If I did have to get on a jet, give me something to drink to get over the shakes. It wasn't from drinking, it was just from being afraid of being up in the air. You never know what you're going to face tomorrow. You don't know what it's going to hold for you. I never in a mil-lion years would have believed that I would be a pilot.

John A. has the utmost respect for Ricky Van, and they have been dear friends since the day they met. John A. especially respected the way he gave credit where it was due.

> Ricky Van had the best voice with a little twang in it than anyone that ever came in The Palace. He made a lot of mon-ey bringing back standard country hits such as "Statue of a Fool." Jack Greene had a hit with it years earlier, and Ricky Van brought it back and made it a number-one hit again.
>
> Let me tell you a little story about that. At the Opry one night, the manager of the Opry told Ricky Van, they've had a lot of requests and they wanted him to sing "Statue of a Fool." Ricky Van said, "I'll have to talk to Jack Greene first." He went over to Jack sitting backstage there at the Opry, and he said, "Jack, they asked me to sing 'Statue of a Fool.'" He said, "Go ahead and sing it, it's alright with me." Ricky Van, made the bravest move I'd ever seen. He went out on that stage and said, "Ladies and gentlemen, I have received a lot of requests for a hit made twenty years ago

by Jack Greene and now it's a hit done by me. I'd like to ask Jack Greene to come out here and sing it with me." Ricky Van brought Jack out on the stage and Jack was beaming. The two of them sang "Statue of a Fool" together that night at the Opry, and I thought that was pure class of Ricky Van. You never do a star's song, if you know the artist is there, and you always ask them first. Ricky Van Shelton is one of the nicest men you will ever meet in your life.

In 2006, Ricky Van called John A. and told him that he was retiring to spend more time with his family. He felt that he had made enough money to live the rest of his life out comfortably, and he was quitting the music business and moving back to Virginia. Ricky Van now spends his days working on his farm. He is an insanely talented painter/artist, enjoys fishing and gardening, and still loves music. Several times a week, Ricky Van goes out back to his private room to pick and sing with a close friend, Bo Heatherley (who Ricky Van jokingly calls his son because they sing so much alike); and sometimes they even record a couple of original tunes. Life is in perspective now, but he will never forget John A. Hobbs and those days at The Palace.

"Walking on stage was always the best," Ricky Van says. "And walking on stage of The Nashville Palace with John A. Hobbs sitting in the audience will always be one of my greatest memories. On that stage is where it all came together for me. In fact, as I continue to gain perspective on my life and career, I thank God for Bettye, who believed in me, and people like John A. Hobbs and Jerry Thompson who believed in me. You've got to have people that believe in you."

CHAPTER TWENTY-TWO

"My God, It *Is* Porter!"

Once he gets on you, he gets on you. You can't get him off you.
Thank God, I don't think he's ever been mad at me,
but I've seen him mad at other people.
Every time, he had a right to be mad.

—TOM POWELL

never had a bouncer in The Palace, because I could always see when trouble was coming. I had to run a few people out, and I had a little scuffle with a few, but in the thirty-five years that I ran The Palace, I only called the police twice. We ran a good, clean place that you could bring your family to. Even Catholic priests and nuns came in there to eat, and I made sure there were no "off-colored" jokes. The only one I had trouble with was Del Reeves. Del would get onstage and go into an "off-colored joke." I called him over and I said, "Del, there are Catholic nuns in the back, so don't use that kind of language in here." Well, he was drinking and started back to using it, so I went up and said, "Ladies and gentlemen, let's give Del Reeves a big hand. He has to be at the Opry in fifteen minutes." He said, "No, I don't!" I said, "Yes, you do!" I took the microphone away from him and got him off the stage.

It has been said about John A. that he is a kind and gentle soul and would do anything for anybody, but just don't ever cross him. John A. was a force to be reckoned with his entire life. If you're his friend, you're his friend for life, but if you've done something wrong, he won't mince any words and he'll tell it to you like it is. He stands up for what is right and is not afraid to confront a man that's done him wrong.

One night we were down at The Palace and two old boys from Texas came in, walked up to the bar, and ordered a drink. They were sitting there at the bar drinking and soon they started to interrupt the pool table, wanting to play. At first, I figured they were heisters trying to take those boys for their money, so I didn't say anything. Wasn't long before they went out to their truck and put on chaps, which in Texas means you are going to try and wreck the place.

As soon as they came back in wearing those chaps, I thought, "This is trouble." I was sitting over in the corner and told the waitress to put two beers up there on the bar for them and place the mugs right in front of me.

I said, "Y'all aren't going to play pool, just take your money up."

One boy said, "We're going in there dancing."

I said, "No you're not; it's couples only."

He looked over and said, "Well, there's other people in there dancing."

"I know what you're doing with those damn western clothes on, and you're not going in there. Now, if y'all want trouble, you're at the right place."

I was going to pop each one of them right in the head with those beer mugs, but they never came over there by me.

One boy asked, "Where's another place at?"

I said, "There's one right down the street."

He said, "I am going down there."

He left this other boy sitting there, and he said, "We ain't goin' to bother you."

I said, "Well, just get on out of here."

John A. was quick to defend his friends like Tom and Christine Powell, who were regulars at The Palace.

Tom Powell was in The Palace one night and some guy told him, "You ain't a writer worth a damn." So, Tom got up to fight and his wife, Christine, ran and got me. Tom said, "I am going to beat the hell out of you!"

I just walked between them and said, "There isn't going to be any fighting in here. Now you sit down, and you sit down."

The man swung at me, and I grabbed him by the tie he was wearing and wrenched it up around my hand. I said, "Now let's go out front," and he swung at me again, so I knocked the hell out of him. Bob from Ohio was there, and I had this guy by the collar. I picked him up and said, "Now, we're going outside."

Tom started to get up from his seat again, and I said, "Don't you get out of that seat!"

I took this guy on over toward the door, and he swung again and I knocked his head off. I knocked him down right in the doorway, and Bob ran over and said, "Boy, don't get up! He's going to kill you!" I said, "Get up, I am getting you out of here."

I carried him out into the parking lot and turned him loose. I said, "Now go on about your business, leave here, and don't ever come back."

I started off, and he turned around and just glazed the back of my head. I hit him hard and knocked him flat in the street. He got up shaking his head, and Bob came over again and said, "Boy, I am telling ya, he's going to kill you if you don't watch out. Stay down and get the hell out of here." He got up and said, "I am leaving, I am leaving!" I told Tom, "The one time I have trouble around here, and you're involved in it."

Tom Powell was the senior editor for thirty-four years of *Amusement Business* and is a very dear friend of John A.'s He spent many hours at The Palace and reflects on the memories of the corner in The Palace.

> Powell: The original corner that John A. sat in with all of his friends was at The Nashville Palace. Back then it was quite a bit different. Actually, where it is now at John A.'s Restaurant doesn't even compare to the way it was

Back row, from left to right: Doug Farris, unknown, Sam Underwood, Orba Maxey, and Tom Powell. Front row, left to right: John A., Tom O'Holleran, and Lou "Pigskin" Hill.

back then. The Palace was just booming, and John A. opened it up as Jerry Reed's Nashville Palace. Over the years, he had Lee Greenwood do shows there, Boxcar Willie, John Michael Montgomery and so many others. Sometimes, I would go through three shifts in there. We had a friend named George that worked for the bank; he'd get there about three o'clock in the afternoon. He'd call me and I'd say, "Damn, George, I don't work for a bank, I'll be over there at four or five." Maybe John would come in, maybe he wouldn't.

We were in there one day, and some guy was sitting where I always sit and it kind of irked me. He was some farmer just sitting there waiting to sell John A. some wooden Indians, and he wasn't even ordering a drink. He was sitting where we always sat and we couldn't sit there as long as he was there. Finally, somebody said, "Well, is John coming in tonight?"

George said, "He told me he would be here at three."

I said, "Well, he told me he'd be here at five."

Another guy piped up and said, "Well, he told me he would be in at six."

This farmer selling wooden Indians sitting over there said, "He told me he'd be here by two."

When John A. finally got there at about seven, he bought all the wooden Indians the guy had on his truck. Then we moved over to our table. The point of that was that in those days, whatever time he told you he was going to be there, it didn't mean anything because he'd tell five people five different times. He'll get there when he got there. So, we used to close the place all of the time.

One time after a fire at The Palace, this man was rebuilding the bar and putting up the racks for the bar glasses. There were about ten of us there and John A. was giving away free drinks to us regulars. The guy installed the racks for the glasses and he and John A. started arguing whether or not the racks were placed too high or too low. John A. said, "Well, I've got a guy here who'll tell you," and he called me over to them.

He said, "What do you think, Tom? Are these shelves too high, or too low?"

I said, to myself, "Please, God, let me say what John A. wants to hear because he doesn't like to be told how to run his business." I said, "What do you think?"

He said, "They're too high."

I said, "You're damn right, they're too high."

Another time a guy came in trying to sell John A. a bar scotch and change it from the one he carried. He said, "I have a guy here that will test it."

I drank a whole bottle and he said, "What do you think?"

I said, "I am not sure yet." So, they opened another bottle.

Once I drank fifty-six scotches in there because I always got them two at a time. You stop and think about it, that's over like seven hours. (That's eight an hour, so one scotch every seven and a half minutes). I'd get ready to leave at three and somebody would come in and I would stay longer.

We had regulars like Pigskin Louie. His real name was Lou Hill. We had a guy named Norm who was a rodeo nut. It wasn't anything like John A.'s Little Palace is now, where I am in there every Friday night. I was in The Nashville Palace every single night, seven nights a week. Minnesota Fats was in there all the time. We never listened to the music, we'd sit in the corner and visit there. One night a big crowd came in there doing a video with John Michael Montgomery and the record people said to me, "Thank, God, you're here, you didn't RSVP." I thought to myself, "Well, I am in here every night." I went out and took a picture and said, "Do you mind if I put somebody else in it?"

They said, "No, who you got?"

I said, "Minnesota Fats."

John Montgomery was more thrilled to see Minnesota Fats than Minnesota Fats was to see John Michael Montgomery, so the picture worked out well.

Minnesota Fats was into car making and used to hang around the old pool players at The Palace a lot. He wasn't really Minnesota Fats, because there was no Minnesota Fats. That was a fictitious name he took from a movie. He told John A. once that he had never even been to Minnesota.

I put him in a bumper pool game with some of my friends at The Palace—Tom Powell and a few others, and he couldn't play and he got beat really bad. I never did put him back in the games again after that.

You know, a lot of big football stars used to come in like Troy Aikman, Bill Wade, and so many more. Bill Wade was a big star back in the early sixties for the Chicago Bears. He played for Vanderbilt and then became the starting quarterback for the Chicago Bears' 1963 NFL championship team. Bill Wade was one of the greatest ball players of his time and became a real champion and a gentleman in football. After he retired, he worked here in Nashville as the PR person for the Third National Bank. Bill used to come to The Palace and sit down, eat, and talk with me. He's a good man and we became good friends.

All the stars came in to The Palace to eat, and John A. advertised it that way. Porter Wagoner came in practically every night because he lived just a few blocks from The Palace in the house with the gate and the two lions in front. He was the nicest guy you could ever sit and talk with and would do anything in the world for you, but he didn't like to be bothered while he was eating.

You know what Porter told me? This was the truth. He said, "Johnny, I don't mind signing autographs or anything, but when I go wash my hands in the bathroom and I am enjoying my food, I don't want to shake hands with people and be signing autographs while I am eating, I don't know where their hands have been."

I said, "Porter, we try to keep everybody away from you."

He said, "I know it and I appreciate it, but I am just telling you why I do it. It's not sanitary."

Most stars don't mind signing autographs if it's the right time, but people don't understand human courtesy. If you see a star, don't run up to them while they are eating. By God, let the man get through eating and then go to him.

Porter came in one night wearing overalls and a ball cap and if you didn't know who he was, you probably wouldn't recognize him at all.

A tourist, a big-mouth woman was sitting at the bar. She said, "Y'all advertise that this is where the stars hang out."

I said, "Yea, that's right."

She said, "Well, I've been here all night and haven't seen a single star."

There were three stars out there at the time, but she didn't recognize them. So, I didn't say anything at first, but she went on running her mouth about it. I said, "Miss, I am going to do you a favor and point you out a star. I want you to promise that you will not go up and bother him, asking for an autograph or anything because he just wants to be left alone."

She said, "Go ahead, ain't nobody in here."

I said, "That's Porter Wagoner over there sitting under Johnny Russell's picture on the wall."

She looked over there and said, "Aw, that's not Porter Wagoner."

So, Porter got through eating, and he walked over to the bar where I was sitting and said, "Johnny, I wanted to tell you that you got the best catfish I've ever eaten."

This woman said, "My god, it *is* Porter!"

He said, "I'll see you later, Johnny."

She said, "That really was Porter!"

I said, "I told you it was," but I didn't tell her there were two more stars still out there.

CHAPTER TWENTY-THREE

Panhandle Slim

*You know the stars of yesterday were a lot of fun
to be with and were always in some kind of a mess.*
—JOHN A. HOBBS

Little Jimmy loved to have a good time, and sometimes we would drive him home at night. We would take him home about seven and his wife used to get so mad at him for being out.

One time he asked me, "You going in to talk to my wife?"

I said, "No, but here's five thousand that you left in my desk."

"Good God, did I leave that money?"

I said, "Yes, it's all yours," and I gave it to him.

He said, "Please go in with me, my wife's gonna be so mad at me!"

Little Jimmy was sitting on the wall outside of his house. With his cowboy outfit on and that big cowboy hat. "Boy, I wish you'd go in there with me."

I said, "Well, I am not going in with you," and I backed out and left him sitting there.

We had a lot of fun in those days. Jimmy Dickens's wife would say something like, "Now, don't you go out to The Palace tonight." He was doing a show for me, so he went to our liquor store and got a small bottle of whiskey, and hid it in the case with his guitar. We brought him home after the show, and I said, "I didn't know he had anything to drink, I told my people not to serve him anything." Later, his wife found out what had happened, and she called me up to tell me that he had hidden the small bottle in his guitar case.

Opening Night for the Wax Museum: Boxcar Willie, Little Jimmy Dickens, and John A., circa 1980.

Little Jimmy and all the Opry stars were down-to-earth; in many ways, they were just like you and me. There is a story that everyone loves to tell about Little Jimmy Dickens. One winter, Little Jimmy was hanging Christmas lights on his house for the season. He climbed onto the roof with a ladder to hang the lights along the gutters and edging of the house. While he was on the roof, the ladder slid sideways and fell to the ground, leaving the country star stranded on his roof.

The weather was cold and his wife was inside the house, unaware that her husband was stuck on the roof. Tour buses regularly drove by the homes of the stars, and Little Jimmy's home was a highlight along the route. While he was trapped on the roof, a tour bus full of waving tourists slowed down while driving by. Little Jimmy stood up waving his arms madly, and it wasn't to say hello to the tourists. Little Jimmy was trying desperately to get their attention for some help.

After several hours and several more tour buses had passed, each time with Little Jimmy waving, he was still trapped on that roof. Cold and tired, he finally started pounding on the roof in the hopes of getting his wife's attention. Finally, a tourist stopped to take pictures. Little Jimmy yelled for him to come through the gate and put the ladder back up for him. Jimmy asked his wife why she didn't come out and help him? She said, "I thought you were nailing shingles on the roof."

Ernest Tubb was known as the Texas Troubadour, and John A. knew that he was a good man, wonderful entertainer, and did so well with people. According to John A., Loretta Lynn would never have been a star if not for Ernest, and he doubts if Elvis Presley would have made it without him, either.

Most people don't know this, but when Elvis first came to Nashville in the early fifties, he tried to get on the Opry. The Opry turned him away, telling him they just didn't think he was good enough. Ernest happened to be standing there, and Elvis walked up to him and asked if he could sing on his *Midnite Jamboree*. Ernest asked Elvis if he had a good voice and Elvis replied, "Yes, I think I can sing." Ernest took a chance and told Elvis to come down to the record shop at seven o'clock that night and he would put him on. So, Elvis sang for the first time in Nashville at Ernest Tubb's Record Store on the *Midnite Jamboree* in 1954. Ernest helped a lot of people out that were down on their luck, although he never had any money himself. Seemed like he could run through it overnight and be broke.

> I opened a western store on one side because western fashion had become real popular. Ernest Tubb was in there one night and we were talking. I liked Ernest and asked him if he would like to own a western store business with me. He

said he didn't have any money to invest, and I told him that I would cut him in with a 40 percent profit just for using his name on it. Specifically, I wanted to use the Texas Troubadour and he agreed. We never had much of an agreement, we just got it written up and signed it.

Ernest came down for the store opening and cut the ribbon. I had Libby, the girl I married, running it for us and it was really successful. Everyone that came into The Palace had a cowboy hat and a pair of boots on, even the bikers. We sold the hell out of hats, boots, and western shirts. We had a Panhandle Slim shirt that was one of the prettiest shirts I ever looked at. It was a little modern, but it was still a western cut and boy did it sell. When we first opened, we went down and nearly bought out the Panhandle Slim factory in Dallas, Texas. I bought pants for eight dollars that we turned and sold for thirty dollars in our store. I bought shirts for five dollars and we were selling them for twenty and we really made some good money.

The funny part happened when I was going to buy Panhandle Slim. The salesman came in, and he was selling over at the nearby Loretta Lynn store. She had two western stores and I leased the property it was on to her, but it wasn't Loretta running it. It had her name on it, but two other people were running it. This sales guy took me to a trailer and showed me all of these clothes. We looked at them to buy, but do you know what he told me? He said, "Mr. Hobbs, I'm going to tell you the truth. I can't deliver for two years to you because I'm backlogged."

I thought, "That doesn't sound right." I said, "Wait a minute, you showed me all these clothes, let me pick them all out, and now you're telling me that I can't order them?"

He said, "Oh, no, Panhandle Slim is booked solid. We can't get to you for two years because we've done promised

Loretta Lynn's we would sell to them." I left him a minute and went over to my liquor store to use the phone in the back room. I called Panhandle Slim directly and said, "I like your line of clothing, and I would like to buy a lot of it for my store."

He said, "Well, we've got plenty in stock."

I said, "In other words, you can sell to me?"

He said, "Yes, but until you establish credit with us, we want cash."

I said, "That's alright, but now I am talking about a large quantity of clothes because we are stocking our entire store."

He said, "I wish you would come down here, we'll even pay your way."

I said, "I don't expect you to do that. I was going to fly down there anyway to see Billy Bob's place."

I didn't think I'd buy that much, but I drew out fifty thousand dollars to carry with me. They brought the owner out there to meet me and I said to him, "I want to ask you something. You tell me you're going to sell me all these clothes, you were overrun on all of it at a big reduced price. Why did your salesman in Nashville tell me that I couldn't buy anything for two years?"

He said, "Did he tell you that?"

I said, "Yes."

"He had no business telling you that."

I said, "You know that's a lawsuit, don't you? I don't want to get my money suing people, but I think you need to know, this man is costing you a lot of business."

He said, "Don't you worry, we'll take care of that. Mr. Hobbs, you can have anything that you want in here." I picked out about fifty thousand dollars' worth and he asked, "Do you want more?"

I said, "Yeah, but I didn't bring that much cash with me."

He said, "I believe your credit is good with us."

I said, "Alright," and I picked out over a hundred thousand dollars' worth on sale. We stocked our western store with an excellent line of Panhandle Slim, right out of Texas.

John A. never treated them like stars, he treated them like friends. He had George Jones living near his place for a while and tried to help him get back on his feet.

George Jones never really stopped drinking, but he quit getting drunk. George lived nearby for five years and frequented The Nashville Palace before he met his wife Nancy. He shared with me one day the reason why he drank. He told me that he couldn't go onstage unless he took a drink.

I said, "What do you mean you can't go onstage?"

He said that he was afraid that the audience wouldn't like him, or that there wouldn't be anybody out there in the audience. He said that he had this feeling all the time like that, so he had to have a small drink before going out onstage.

John A., Chief Joe Casey, "Skull" Schulman, George Jones, and Pee Wee Johnson at The Palace.

I said, "Good God-Almighty, after forty years onstage you look like you could just walk out there," but he couldn't do it, he just couldn't walk out there.

Waylon Jennings came into The Palace one night asking for George. I took Waylon back there and George was sitting by himself. Boy, George got down to where he didn't even weigh 115 pounds. I told Waylon that he looked bad and he went on over and sat down with him. He told George that he wanted him to go get himself straightened out now. He told him to go to rehab and get treated to get off this stuff. George just replied, "Yeah, yeah, yeah."

Waylon counted out twenty-five thousand dollars in hundred-dollar bills and laid them on the table. I told the waitress to bring me a sack and I put the money in it and wrapped a rubber band around it. Waylon said, "Y'all going to see that he gets home with it?" I said, "Yeah, I am going to be damn sure he gets home with it!"

Johnny Cash's driver, Big George, was outside. I said, "I want you to do me a favor. They are going to drive George home and you go with him. I want you to put this bag in his freezer. Put him in bed and be sure it's locked when you leave."

I called George the next day and told him to look in his freezer for the bag of money and he told me he had already found it. A few weeks later, George came in The Palace and he didn't have any money to buy a beer. I gave him a beer and asked, "George, what happened to that damn twenty-five thousand Waylon gave you?"

He said, "I bought a car with it. Come on out here and see it."

I went out front and he had bought a Nova, Chevrolet, the cheapest car on the road. Back in those days it wouldn't have cost seven thousand dollars brand new. It didn't even have hubcaps or a radio, but it had a heater. The car was plain without chrome or anything. I said, "George, that car didn't cost over seven thousand dollars, where's your money?"

He said, "I got a lot of friends, so I guess I just went through it."

Two weeks later he was out at The Palace without the car and never did go in for treatment. I tell you, George made a remarkable recovery and I think his wife Nancy and Pee Wee Johnson had a lot to do with it. Pee Wee got him halfway straightened out and then Nancy met him. He was pretty straight, 95 percent of the time. He was really an improved man for the last twenty-plus years that he lived.

CHAPTER TWENTY-FOUR

Touched by an Angel

You're going to be stunned, Libby.
When you look down at that church, it's going to be packed.
My friends are your friends, and your friends are mine.
—JOHN A. HOBBS

After Mary and John divorced, he met the love of his life, Elizabeth Ann Murphy. "Libby" was a beautiful lady inside and out and had such a sweet personality that everyone loved. You never met a kinder soul, and she was always up for going anywhere and so much fun to be around. Libby exuded class and it seemed that they adored each other. John A. first met Libby while she was running the Loretta Lynn's Western Wear store near The Nashville Palace. After work, she used to come in to The Palace for a drink and to socialize. They just really hit it off and for the first time in his life, John A. had a woman to go places with him. She had her own house near Percy Priest Lake and John A. was living at the Fiddler's Inn in Music Valley. She had a son, Mike, and a daughter, Kim, and John A. treated them as he did his own family.

185

Elizabeth "Libby" Ann Murphy

They dated for five years before marrying and building a home together on Pennington Bend. His son, Joe Hobbs, was the builder of the house, where John A. still resides today. The house was built with high ceilings and a den large enough to enjoy. It was modern when they built it with all the upgrades in the kitchen. Gorgeous solid redwood cabinets and stainless-steel appliances. The saltwater pool was added in 1994, and it is the most serene and peaceful location you can imagine, and yet it is just minutes to Music Valley Drive.

John A. was at a point in his life where he had the boys to help run the businesses, and he had the time and money to travel more and the two of them never hesitated to go somewhere.

When he and Libby did go, they truly enjoyed each other's company.

> Libby, she was a pretty woman, a beautiful lady. She never thought she was pretty, but she was, and she had a personality. You know, I never called Libby in the years that we were together and said, "Let's go somewhere," that she didn't get ready. She never said, "I can't make it or anything like that," and she was always ready to go. I would call her up and say, "Lib, let's fly to New York," and she would simply ask, "What time are you leaving?" We would fly up for three days to see the opening of a Broadway play or something like that. I also liked visiting San Francisco, so I'd say let's fly up to San Francisco for four or five days and stay, but I was making good money then.

John A. admired Libby for her many genuine qualities, but especially her appreciation for everything. Libby never threw money away because she had grown up without it in Butcher Holler. Loretta Lynn and Libby were the same age and attended school together, beginning in the first grade. When school let out, the two girls used to play together and pick up coal that had fallen off the trains coming out of the nearby coal mines. They would get sacks and drag them along, picking up coal as they went. When they got to where they could hardly drag the load, they would take it to the house, dump it out, and go back for more. They would gather enough coal to heat the house during the winter months. They knew what hard times were and never took anything for granted. They only went through grade school together, but Libby and Loretta stayed friends for life. Libby used to go on Loretta's tour bus, and they stayed in touch quite often on the phone. John A. and Libby were invited to Loretta's house in Hurricane Mills,

Tennessee numerous times, and they said that she was as down-to-earth as anybody they ever knew.

> We were lucky enough to meet the people we've met considering where we came from. We've met a lot of famous people in our lives, but I treated them just like I would anybody else, and they treated me the same.

Libby and John A. were inseparable and lived life to the fullest together with trips, special occasions, and building their home together in the bend. For every event, Libby was right there on John A.'s arm. He changed her life forever, and she changed his as well. When she was dying with cancer, she told John A. how she felt about their precious time together and all of the unforgettable memories she held of being his wife.

> In 2009, Libby was diagnosed with cancer and was real sick. Doctor Birdwell called me and said, "Johnny, you want to come out and see me? I need to talk to you."
> I said, "You can tell me over the phone."
> "Can you take what I am fixing to say?"
> I said, "Yeah."
> He said, "Libby is dying," and he said, "She probably won't live more than six months. She's got cancer really bad."
> I took her to a doctor out at Vanderbilt to see if he could do anything for her, but he said it was too late, she was already eaten up with it. She only lived about six weeks after that, but let me tell you what Libby told me five days before she died. We were out there by ourselves at the nursing home and she said, "Sit down here, I want to talk to you." I sat down on the hospital bed with her and was holding her hand. She said, "Johnny, I want to tell you something. Being married to you was like a roller coaster. We were out doing something all the time, and I never knew where I was going

or who I was going to meet. I never dreamed we would meet the people we met. I am from Butcher Holler and was never well educated. My God, I didn't know what to say to people when we would meet them, so I just stood back, but you could talk to people." She said, "I remember when we went to the Governor's Mansion and met upstairs privately with Al Gore. The only thing I could think of, was that I wish my mother and daddy could see us sitting there with the vice president of the United States, just talking. I was so scared, and didn't know what to say or do, but I tried to carry on a conversation. You and him just carried on and kidded and talked. I never have forgotten that. You could talk to people, the mayor, the governor, whomever, and I couldn't. You talked with sense and not a lot of crap, and you didn't want anything from them."

She went over the other things like having breakfast with Gene Autry, Dale Evans, and Roy Rogers, and wishing that her brothers had lived long enough to have seen her with them because they used to play like they were Gene Autry and Roy Rogers all the time as kids. Libby said, "Johnny, you've got more friends than any man I ever knew in my whole lifetime. You amaze me. You get along with everybody, and if you don't like them you walk off and leave them. That's a gift. Most people stand there and argue, but you just walk off, shake your head, and let it go. When I die, there probably won't be anybody at my funeral." I said, "You're going to be stunned. When you look down at that church, it's going to be packed." She said, "You really think so?" I said, "Yes! My friends are your friends, and your friends are mine."

Libby passed away on June 15, 2009 and John A. was right, the church was packed full of people from all over who came to pay their respects. Even the Speaker of the House called a recess in business matters so that he and others could attend the service. She was greatly loved, and there wasn't a dry eye in the place.

Touched by an Angel

I'll see you one day soon again my love,
Please put in a good word for me, when God you finally see,
Because I know you're going to heaven,
I'm just not sure about me.
But when the Good Lord gets to meet you,
He will know I'm OK, too,
Because I have been touched by an Angel,
And that Angel is you!
I've been touched by an Angel,
I've been blessed with your love,
How can I ever repay you?
I thank God above.
For sending me an Angel to share my life,
I've been touched by an Angel, and the Angel is you, my wife.
—John A. Hobbs

CHAPTER TWENTY-FIVE

"Can You Sing?"

If you don't have a helping hand, you can't go anywhere.
It's really the truth, you have to have some help.
—JOHN A. HOBBS

John A. was known to help people in every way imaginable. He was more worried about the common man than anyone else, and he enjoyed giving back and refused to receive any recognition for his good deeds. In fact, most of his acts of generosity went entirely unknown outside the grateful recipient. There are countless stories of John A. providing free hotel accommodations for years, hospitality in his personal guest house, many a meal and free drink to friends and visitors, parties have been hosted, fundraisers held, solid business advice given, anonymous donations for church needs, and on and on. John A. has held his hand out to help his fellow man all of his life and he considers himself lucky that he can do what he does. This is just one of the many reasons, people love and respect him as much as they do.

I was in The Palace one night and a young man came up to me by the door and didn't know who I was. He said, "What do you have to do to get onstage here?"

He was ragged and poor looking. I said, "Can you sing?"

191

He said, "Yeah."

I said, "Where are you from?"

"Down in Alabama, but let me tell you what happened to me. Me and my wife were driving up here today, and we don't have any money. This car went to bumping me, trying to wreck me, and I finally made it to an off ramp and pulled into a service station. Luckily, they kept going." I said, "You did the right thing, just getting out of the way."

"They tore my bumper off my truck, and I wired it back up."

I looked over and he had an old truck and a pile of junk.

"Son, is that all the clothes you have?"

He said, "Yes, sir."

I said, "Wait a minute."

I put him up there onstage and let him sing. He wasn't a star, but he was pretty good. He had old ragged blue jeans on and an old dirty shirt, so when he came off, I said, "I want you to meet me in the morning at Ernest Tubb's Western Shop. We own it, and I want you to be there at eleven o'clock."

The next morning, I took him in that western store and I bought him a new pair of boots, sport coat, the whole western outfit. He was beaming. I gave him a room at the hotel for two nights, and that night he came in dressed up. He got up onstage and he did a decent job, but I've never have seen or heard from him again. I don't know whatever happened to him. People like that, I enjoy doing something for, because they are the kind of people that are hard workers, and you could tell just by looking at them.

This other young kid from Georgia was at the Fiddler's Inn one night with his wife. He was asking how much it would be to park his pickup with the camper on it and sleep in his truck on his honeymoon. She told him it would be ten dollars and he replied that he didn't have that much money.

I said, "Son, is that your truck out there?"

He said, "Yes, sir. I just got married this morning, and we are on our honeymoon."

I said, "Look, you're not going to sleep in your truck," and I gave them a nice room at the hotel. I said, "I want you to come down to The Palace tonight, and I am going to feed you, and you will have a wedding party."

They came down there that night and, aw, he thanked me, and him and his wife cried. She was a little old country girl. They had a big time, and I let him get up and sing a little. They sent me a nice letter after it was all over and said, "You made our honeymoon for us and we sure appreciate it!" A lot of them came by like that, and I could never turn them down. Libby used to say, "You don't know whether they are real or phonies." I said, "I don't really care. If they tell a story like they tell, I am going to give to them anyway."

One night we were sitting out at The Palace. I never will forget this, I looked up and there's this kid standing there with a T-shirt on. He said, "Mr. Hobbs. I got my baby out in the car, and I don't have any money to buy food and my baby's hungry. Could you give me a little money to buy a little milk?" I pulled out a hundred dollars and gave it to him. I said, "Son, go buy him some baby food or whatever he needs. Call me if you need more."

He said, "I'll take care of him. Thank you so much," and he cried.

Libby and our friends turned around, they were sitting there. They said, "How do you know that's not a 'flim-flam' and he doesn't even have a baby out there?"

I said, "If he doesn't, I don't want to know about it."

They laughed and said, "You really didn't give a damn if he was lying." I said, "I just want to see that kid fed."

One night a lady came in and asked to see John A., and she came around there to the corner where he was sitting. She was a daughter of a friend in the entertainment business, and she told him that she hadn't eaten in a week. Drugs had gotten to her and her parents had thrown her out of the house. She said, "I've been drinking too much and I need to get off the drugs, but I am starving and weak and need something to eat."

John A. called the waitress over and told her to give the young lady anything she wanted to eat, but no alcohol. She ordered steak and catfish and devoured both orders and drank iced tea. She came over when she finished and thanked John A. for the food and disappeared. She never came back, and he never did hear whatever happened to her.

CHAPTER TWENTY-SIX

Tennessee Waltz

I always asked stars if they wrote a hit song, how they wrote it.
There's a story to every one of those songs.
—JOHN A. HOBBS

John A. was always fascinated with how the stars ended up writing the songs they did. He loved to hear the stories behind each one, and had ample opportunity to sit with some of the best songwriters in the business. One of his favorite things was to listen to an artist telling the audience a little history behind the song they were about to perform.

I used to go out to Las Vegas to see Frank Sinatra, Dean Martin, and all of them. One thing I liked about Frank Sinatra—I saw five of his shows—is he would tell the audience about the song he was about to sing. When he was going to do a song like "My Way," he would preface it by saying, "I am going to do this song with lyrics written by Paul Anka, who is a dear friend of mine." I also watched Boxcar Willie perform on many occasions, and he used to tell who wrote the song. I think that anybody who is in the singing business or entertaining, should tell who wrote that song for the people. I

195

used to ask every star I met, "How did you write that song?"
Nine out of ten times they wrote it about something that
happened to them.

Most people don't remember Pee Wee King, whose father
managed Gene Autry. Pee Wee co-wrote the "Tennessee Waltz."
John A. asked him one day about the story behind the writing of
the famous song, and Pee Wee was more than happy to share it.
He told John A. that in late December 1946, he was driving a '42
pickup truck back to Nashville from Little Rock, Arkansas with
his buddy, Redd Stewart and some of their band's equipment.
They were coming through Memphis, but had tuned the radio to
a St. Louis station and they were playing a waltz. Pee Wee asked
Redd why nobody had ever written a Tennessee waltz? They
write about St. Louis and all those other cities, but nobody ever
writes about Tennessee. So, he said, "Let's write one!" All they
had to write on in the cab of that truck was a matchbook cover.
They tore the matches off and went to work. Pee Wee told John
A. that they would hum a little bit, then write a little ... hum a
little bit, then write a little bit. They had to get it right the first
time because they didn't have any more room to write. Pee Wee
drove to Jackson, Tennessee where Redd took over the driving,
and Pee Wee finished writing the rest of the song. It needed to be
polished up, but overall, they thought it was pretty good.

On Monday morning, they presented the song to Fred Rose,
who had teamed up with Grand Ole Opry star Roy Acuff to
create the first Nashville-based publishing company. Mr. Rose
adjusted the first line, cleaned it up a little, and held onto it. In
December 1947 Pee Wee King's Golden West Cowboys were
finally able to record the song and released it in January of 1948.
Pee Wee thought the song wasn't going to be a hit, but in 1950

Patti Page came to Nashville and fell in love with the song. She picked it up and made it a number-one hit, and eventually it became the state song and is now well known throughout the world.[29]

We were lucky we met a lot of good people. The Opry stars were all good people. Johnny Russell was good-hearted and would do anything for anyone. He wrote some of the biggest hits there ever was. I asked Johnny Russell one time how he wrote "Act Naturally." You know, he wrote that thing driving from San Francisco to Los Angeles, and he had a part in a movie. He said that he was riding along and got to thinking that he was going to be a big star now. He started singing, just talking to himself. He pulled over to the side of the road and wrote that song.

It knocked around for a year or two, and then everybody recorded it and it made a big hit. He never met the Beatles, but they recorded his song, made it a number-one hit, and sold millions of copies. Then Loretta Lynn, Charlie Pride, and Buck Owens recorded it and sold millions more. That song has become a national stand-by song like "For the Good Times." That song is always going to be popular. Then he wrote two or three more good songs, like his hit, "I've Got No Reason to Go Home Now." He went through divorce court, came out and got in his car and said, "Hell, I've got no reason to go home now." He said, "Ooh, that'd make a good song," and he started singing. He sat there in his car and wrote that damn song in front of the courthouse and it became a number-one hit. He also wrote "Rednecks, White Socks, and Blue-Ribbon Beer." Jimmy Carter's brother, Billy Carter, came over one night and told us that his brother hated that damn song and he was president at that time. We all got a laugh.

John A. found some of his dearest friends through the contacts that he made in Music Valley at The Palace. These friends included not only entertainers, but also Major League Baseball players, umpires, and managers. He recalls some of the best times going to Florida for Spring Training.

Me, Johnny Russell, and Boxcar Willie were close friends. We used to go to Spring Training together. One time, we went down to Spring Training, and Boxcar and I are just walking along and this lady ran up to him said, "I know who you are! You're big star!"

He said, "Who am I?"

She said, "You're Waylon Jennings!"

He said, "No! What about Boxcar Willie?"

She said, "You can't fool me, Waylon, I know who you are." She gave him a piece of paper and he signed it Waylon Jennings. He laughed and shook his head. "I couldn't convince her that I was really Boxcar Willie."

We had a lot of fun at Spring Training in Florida. The first night we were there, fifteen of us all went to dinner. I said, "I'll get it tonight," and the check was seven hundred and fifty dollars, and I left a generous tip. The next night at dinner, Boxcar said, "Don't pull your billfold out, I'm getting the check tonight." So, he's telling us all that his daughter told him that you tip one dollar per head for how many people are at the table. The bill came to almost eight hundred dollars, and he didn't hesitate to pay. We were all sitting there and I thought, "Oh, God, we eat here a lot, and I wasn't going to get out with just a fifteen-dollar tip." So, I put a twenty under my plate and noticed Tommy put a twenty under his plate, too. Nobody wanted Boxcar to see because it would embarrass him, but ole Box left the waitress a fifteen-dollar tip for an eight-hundred-dollar dinner. So, we left and never said a word to him about it.

John A. and Boxcar used to go to Florida and meet up with their mutual friend and Major League Baseball umpire, Joe West for Spring Training.

West: I was introduced to John A. by Boxcar Willie. You know that the network of people in Nashville is like a family, some good brothers and sisters, some bad. Boxcar was a true peach of a person, and he was a starving musician trying to plug in a trailer on one sub-freezing night outside the old Fiddler's Inn Campground, and John A. found him out in the weather and went inside Fiddler's Inn Motel and got him a room for the night. Didn't hurt that John A. owned the hotel. The next night, Boxcar walked into The Palace and asked John A. if he could "play" for his room and the rest is history. Boxcar sold over three million records on infomercials, and he and John A. became lifelong friends.

John A. was instrumental in getting Boxcar on *Hee Haw* and introducing him to Roy Acuff. Boxcar became a kind of cult hero with his train whistle and old country covers. He became a member of the Grand Ole Opry and was the original theater owner in Branson, Missouri. The Boxcar Willie Theatre and The Boxcar Willie Museum were original landmarks in Branson, and none of it would have happened if John A. hadn't gotten an old hobo out of the cold. Hobbs and his wife Libby attended Boxcar's funeral in Branson. Every flag in town was at half-mast, and as the funeral procession went to the cemetery all of the employees from the other theaters were on the streets of Branson with their heads bowed and their hands over their hearts. The trains were stopped on the tracks nearby and as the hearse passed slowly by, they sounded their train whistles in salute. I know this because I was one of the pall bearers.

John A. thought Joe West was a lot of fun to go out with. They always had a big time wherever they went. Joe has an outgoing and fun-loving personality and can strike up a conversation with anybody. Joe is also a country singer and songwriter, and everyone nicknamed him Cowboy Joe.

> We used to go down to a little western club, and Joe and Boxcar would get up and sing. They would take turns getting up to sing, and we would have a big time. I'll tell you one about Joe West. One time he was at Dodger Stadium, when Walter O'Malley was still living. Joe is a big man, he's six-foot-four and probably weighs two hundred fifty pounds. Well, he came out walking across the field toward home plate with his signature cowboy boots on. Walter O'Malley owned the team and was up in the press box at the time. He looks down on the field and said, "Who is that on my field with cowboy boots on?" The guy next to him said, "That's the umpire, Joe West." He said, "Ooh! Let him walk."

Boxcar came up the hard way, living, literally, a few feet from the KD railroad tracks in a small three-room tool shed. He was born Lecil Travis Martin in Sterratt, Texas, and later took the stage name Boxcar Willie. The highlight of his music career was being invited by Roy Acuff to sing on the Grand Ole Opry. Roy really liked Boxcar and they became dear friends. In 1981, Boxcar became a member of the Opry, which was a lifelong dream come true for him. In 1985, he bought a theater across the street from Roy Clark's and settled into the Branson community with his wife and children.[30]

When Boxcar bought his theater out there in Branson, Missouri, he thought he would go broke. He paid a million dollars for it. He called me up and he said, "What do you think?" I said, "I think you're going to make a lot of money." He said, "I am buying it, but it's the first time I've ever been in debt. If I go broke, I'll just come back and work for you." So, he'd kid and cut up, but he was a dear friend and he made it just fine out there.

Boxcar was a member of the Grand Ole Opry, and he and John A. paid a visit to Roy Acuff backstage in his dressing room and received a message that they would both never forget.

Roy Acuff was really sick when me and Boxcar went backstage to his dressing room one night. I never will forget, Roy took my hand and said "Johnny, keep playing country music. You're the only one in Nashville who's playing the true country music, so keep it alive." He turned to Boxcar and he said, "Box, when I die, don't let the 'Wabash Cannonball' die with

John A. and Boxcar Willie.

me. Promise me you will play it every night at your show."
Boxcar called Roy, "King." He said, "King, I promise you, I will
play it every night." Roy died a year later in 1992 from congestive heart failure at the age of eighty-nine. Boxcar called
me and said, "Johnny, the King died. When are they going to
bury him?"

I said, "You're too late, they are burying him right now."

"Well, are we going to have a memorial?"

I said, "Yeah, on Friday night, and Ricky Skaggs is heading
it up. Box said, "Ooh boy, I'll be in for it."

Roy Acuff put it in his last will and testament that he
wanted to be buried as quickly as they could bring him to
the cemetery. I received a call saying if I was going out to the
funeral that morning, I had better get out there right now. I
went out there, and there were maybe twenty people or less
gathered. There was a poor looking kid out there playing an
old guitar, I never will forget it. He was just a young kid and
he sat on the next tombstone over, when they were burying
Roy, and he was playing Roy's songs in tribute. In memory
of Roy, I ask Dianne Sherrill to sing "The Wabash Cannonball" two or three times a week at the club. I think of Roy
because he was a fine man. He was good for the Opry, good
for Nashville, and just good for everything. He was the kind
of man that brought respect to the Opry, and he didn't want
anything to make people think differently.

In 1996 Boxcar was diagnosed with leukemia. After three
hard-fought years, he succumbed to cancer on April 12, 1999,
dying in Branson, Missouri.[31]

CHAPTER TWENTY-SEVEN

The Stars
Came Out

You know, out of all the people at the Opry, I never met a bad one.
They were all nice, always polite, and never pushed the crowd away.
I have personally seen them sign autographs
as long as the fans were standing there.

—JOHN A. HOBBS

John A. was on the Academy of Country Music Board quite a few years, and even before he was on the board, he attended many of the award ceremonies in support of his various friends. John A. and company would go out to Los Angeles a day or two early, and when the stars started coming in, they would all congregate in the hotel bar. They would kid and cut up with some of the biggest names in country music, which were just good ole friends to them.

> George Strait sat at our table one night and we all had a good time. He got to signing autographs and signed his cowboy hat and gave it to this woman. Without his hat, he looked entirely different and nobody recognized him sitting there. I told him, "George, you should never wear a

hat, they don't know who you are." Brooks and Dunn, Lorrie Morgan, Reba McIntyre, and Boxcar Willie were all sitting there, and we had the whole bar almost to ourselves. We used to sit backstage, and they would give me a table right there where the stars went onstage. I would let some of my friends sit there with me, and the stars would all sit down at our table until it was time for them to go on. We met a lot of the big, big superstars that way.

I went to the awards show the year they gave Keith Whitley an award. He had the prettiest green suit I ever looked at. He and Lorrie Morgan were married and he came down and sat down with me, and we were kidding him about giving out an award. I was on the board of directors, and he said, no way would he go out there and do that. Lorrie knew we were joking with him, and she laughed about it, and we had a lot of fun. Just a few weeks later, Keith drank a fifth of whiskey and died from alcohol poisoning. What a tragic loss that was.

Roy Rogers starred in over a hundred films and most of those were filmed along with his third wife, Dale Evans. He was known as the "King of Cowboys" and fans favored his famous palomino horse, Trigger, and his German Shepard, Bullet. Dale Evans and Roy met in his very first film, and he died from congestive heart failure just after their fiftieth wedding anniversary in 1998.[32] While in Los Angeles for the awards show, a friend of John A.'s called him up and invited him to a breakfast meetup with Roy Rogers. The day of the awards show, they took a limo out where Roy Rogers lives, which is about thirty-five miles outside of the city. Roy was running late that morning coming from a doctor's appointment, so John A. and company had the opportunity to sit and visit with Roy's wife Dale Evans and their son, Dusty.

A half-hour later, Roy came in, wearing a jogging suit and a ball cap and no one recognized him. Dale said, "You have to get your sugar flow, let's go get something to eat." He said, "Let's go to the Hotcake, I love hotcakes. Y'all want to go with us?" We went in the restaurant which was a lot like a Denny's, and they pulled the tables together and we sat there for four hours. Roy Rogers was the nicest guy and not a soul in the room recognized him or asked for an autograph. Dale was sitting there looking like she came out of a showroom. Her hair was perfect and everything was just so, and we all became dear friends.

Many consider Gene Autry to be the greatest western star of all time. He gained fame as the original singing cowboy in the 1930s and composed some of the biggest hits of all time including, "Back in the Saddle Again," "Rudolph the Red-Nosed Reindeer," and "That Silver-Haired Daddy of Mine." He was also the first

John A., Tom Powell, and Gene Autry.

artist to have a gold record, and in 1940 he was one of the most sought-after actors.[33]

> A day later we went to a ballgame and were sitting up in the box and we could see in to Gene Autry's box. He owned the Los Angeles Angels baseball team. Well, he had waiters in there with tuxedos on. This waiter comes in our box and says, "Mr. Hobbs? Mr. Autry would like for you to join him in his box." So, sure enough we went over there, and he had a whole house up there. He had bedrooms, he had living rooms, and a box where he could watch the ballgame. Now, Gene was the kind of guy, that when his team came to bat, he would get out his field glasses and watch every move. Then when it was over, he would get up and talk to you, but you couldn't talk to him at all while play was going on. Sam Lovullo had a son Torey playing for Gene Autry and the Angels. He hit a grand slam home run with the bases loaded. I said, "Good God, that's Sam Lovullo's son." He said, "Who?" I said, "Torey Lovullo, his daddy produced *Hee Haw*. He said, "I know Sam!" We laughed and we talked a little bit, and he sat back down. We stayed over there until the sixth or seventh inning and then returned to our box. Autry sent all of the his food over to our box and it was enough food to feed an army.

CHAPTER TWENTY-EIGHT

Last Call at The Palace

*If there were no valleys of sadness and death,
we could never really appreciate the sunshine
of happiness on the mountaintop.*
—ROY ROGERS

John A. has lived a long life, and as a result he has seen the changes that life can bring, both good and bad. He has seen the creation and crumble of many a business around him, and sadly he has met and lost a lot of friends and family along the way. He seems to embrace change and expect it, preparing for the future rain even when he is basking in the sunshine of today. His resiliency is incredible, really, but one of his toughest losses was that of his long-time business partner, Louis McRedmond.

In August of 1997, Louis was in the hospital after having a heart attack and he'd been real sick. You know what he told me? I never will forget this. The Tuesday before he died, I waited until the family had left and went out to Saint Thomas Hospital about ten o'clock at night to see him. He was lying flat on his back in his hospital bed without a pillow under him, staring at the ceiling. He didn't even know I was standing there in the doorway. I was there two or three minutes before I grabbed his hand and said, "Hey, partner, what in the hell are you doing?"

He said, "Aw, Johnny. I was just thinking about us." He said, "You know what? We've been partners for years, and we've never had a cross word. We made a lot of money and we really did well. I want to tell you something. You're the best business-man I've ever met in my life. Without you, we couldn't have made it, and I am thrilled to death that we got together when we did. I wanted to thank you for everything." I didn't realize he was that close to death.

He was released from the hospital that Friday on Boxcar Willie's birthday. We were having a party for Boxcar that night at the Ramada, and Louis made it out there with the help of his son, Louie Jr. I said, "Come on in! I am glad you got out today." He said, "Boy, I am glad to be here!" Boxcar looked awful, too. He was really sick and dying with cancer and didn't have but another year to live. I thought Louis was doing better, but when he left that night, I never saw him again.

Boxcar's birthday party—John A., Louis McRedmond, and Boxcar Willie.

That Sunday morning on August 10, 1997, Louis got up to go to church and while shaving, fell over dead. He was eighty-four and died in the same house he was born in on Massman Drive in Nashville.

Opryland USA was ranked thirtieth in attendance in the annual ranking of U.S. amusement parks in 1996. Although it was generating revenue during its one-hundred-forty-day season, it was declining in attendance each year of operation. The hope was that a year-round outlet mall—with more than two hundred shops, restaurants, and entertainment venues—would create up to five thousand permanent jobs and annual state and local tax revenues of thirty million dollars.[34] When Opryland closed in 1997, John A. had already sold off his hotels and followed with selling the museums and, after many glorious years, the famed Nashville Palace, too. The Rudy family became the sole owners of The Nashville Palace, buying out their partners and outbidding Gaylord and Wal-Mart for the property which included the strip mall. They closed the legendary honkytonk, but John A. saved the memorabilia and the stories that go along with it.

> Then of course, they closed the park, and it hurt a lot of the surrounding businesses. It didn't wipe us out because I sold a lot before the "official" closing in 1997. Plus, our buildings were designed so if the business we put in there didn't survive, it wouldn't take much to convert them into something else that will make money. We only had ten million into the Ramada when we sold it to Opryland. They offered sixteen million dollars and I said, "Y'all bought it!" I sold The Palace after many years of running it because Nashville was changing, and it was time to get out of it.

Hobbs Highway dedication. Joe Hobbs, John A., Johnny C, and Ronnie Hobbs.

The closing night at The Palace was well attended. Keeping with tradition, it was a star-studded event. The night was held to honor John A. Hobbs for all those years of memories and for all that he had done for country music and for the communities of Music Valley Drive and Nashville. The state representative had a dedication to make, which would memorialize John A. Hobbs forever in Davidson County. Voice impressionist, comedian, and song writer, Johnny Counterfit had the honor of introducing the state representative, Ben West Jr., who made the following statement with John A. sitting in the audience:

> "Ladies and gentlemen, we're here tonight to honor the Hobbs family, and the patriarch, John A. Hobbs. I bring the

state legislature, a House Joint Resolution, that you need to listen to. House Joint Resolution number 180, a resolution, ladies and gentlemen, to name a certain segment of State Route 155 Briley Parkway, in Davidson County, in honor of John A. Hobbs. Let me read it further because I did not say the John A. Hobbs Memorial.

Whereas; from time to time, the members of this General Assembly have seen fit to name certain highways and bridges in honor of those exemplary citizens and public servants who have contributed significantly to the growth and prosperity of their respective communities, and whereas; no Tennessean is more deserving of this honor than John A. Hobbs of Davidson County. Whereas; born February 11, 1928 in Nashville, John A. grew up in West Nashville and attended local schools. A noted entrepreneur, having been the proprietor of Fiddler's Inn, The Nashville Palace and a number of a museums in the Music Valley area, and Whereas; Mr. Hobbs is a person of impeccable morals and irreproachable integrity. Ladies and gentlemen, politicians don't lie. An irreproachable integrity with work to establish a vital future for the people of this community. Whereas; in appreciation of his meritorious service to Metropolitan Nashville Davidson County community, it is the wish of this body to name a certain segment of State Route 155 Briley Parkway to permanently commemorate John A. Hobbses bountiful life of purpose and commitment. Now therefore, be it resolved that the House of Representatives of the 104th General Assembly of the State of Tennessee, the city concurring, that the segment known as State Route 155 Briley Parkway, on Pennington Bend, commencing with such routes interaction with Two Rivers Parkway and proceeding North on Briley Parkway to the Cumberland River, in Davidson County, is hereby designated as the John A. Hobbs Highway!"

Now forty years since John A. opened The Nashville Palace in 1977, the Cumberland Hospitality Group with John A.'s grandson, Barrett Hobbs, at the helm, are now owners once again. Although it is not in the exact location as it was, much of the original memorabilia is displayed there. Keeping with the Hobbs tradition, there is great atmosphere, delicious food, and live music every night. Once again, it is the place to hang out in Music Valley. John A. has been seen hanging out there again lately and one waitress exclaimed, "You're Mr. Hobbs? Wow, you're like folklore around here!"

CHAPTER TWENTY-NINE

Politics

I like people, but the only ones I can't put up with
are the ones that think they are really something better
and they're not. I don't have any time
for these kinds of people.

—JOHN A. HOBBS

ohn A. found himself in politics by accident, but realized also it was good for business to have friends in high places. When he lobbied for improved roads or street lighting, name changes, or zoning issues, things went a lot smoother if you had a hand in politics along the way. The last Saturday of every month, John A. hosts a free breakfast for friends and family, and it is always filled with politicians, too. Especially around election time. John A. has supported many people who were running for office with fundraising parties and substantial financial donations. He made a difference in the campaigns of Tennessee Governor Ned McWherter and Senator Al Gore, Jr., and they became good friends as well.

Al Gore was a really nice man, and when he was senator, I held a big party for him to raise money. We had him onstage singing the "Tennessee Waltz" and had a lot of fun. I didn't know I was going to meet President Clinton when he came to Nashville. The Secret Service called me up and told me they had tickets for me. So, I carried four of my buddies with me, but when we got to the door and they ushered me over to one side. I knew there was something up. After the president and vice president spoke, the Secret Service came to get me. We walked through a side door and into the back with a huge drape across the room. I was first in line, and this woman took my name tag off and stuck it on the inside of my coat pocket as they signaled for me. I stepped through that curtain and there was President Clinton and Vice President Al Gore with the governor. I heard Al Gore tell the president who I was and how I owned The Nashville Palace right across the street from where they were staying. He mentioned how I helped him a lot with his campaign when he was running for office. Clinton smiled and said, "Hey, Johnny! How are you doing?" Just like I'd known him for years. He had more personality than anybody I'd ever met, and he put his arm around me and we walked to the platform for a picture. We stood there and talked awhile and I said, "Mr. President, you know you have a guy here that tries to sing?" He responded, "Do you think I'd have a vice president that couldn't sing?" I said, "Well, you got one, but he better keep his day job," and we all laughed.

One of the things that John A. is proud of, is the fact that people from all walks of life have come to him over the years for advice in all matters, not just business. College graduates, bikers, and others call him frequently asking if they can come by the office to talk off-the-cuff. One thing everyone knows in town is that John A. will give you solid advice and tell you what you need to hear and not just what you want to hear. He is a man who will tell you the truth about anything, and his word is as good as gold. That reputation has even the highest of offices in the land calling him for a few words of encouragement and advice.

I really knew Al Gore when he was working as a reporter for *The Tennessean* newspaper. He was elected to Congress and then became a senator, and finally the vice president of the United States. Al Gore called me one day, from Washington, D.C., when he was vice president. My secretary answered the phone and she said, "Mr. Hobbs, Mr. Hobbs! You're not going to believe it, but the vice president of the United States is on the phone for you!" I said, "How do you know it isn't a joke?" She said, "It's him, I know it is."

I picked up the phone, and I always called him Mr. Vice President, and I said, "Mr. Vice President, how are you doing?"

He said, "I want to ask you something. Is there anything you can tell me I am doing wrong up here? Something you could help me with? What do you think I need to do?"

I said, "Mr. Vice President, I want to tell you something. Whatever you're doing, keep doing it, because you're doing a fantastic job. People respect you, and I think you're doing an outstanding job."

He said, "Well, is there something you think I need to know or anything? I am calling up a few close friends just to find out if there is something that could help me."

I said, "Whatever you're doing, keep it up."

We hung up and I thought, "You know, I wish I had taped that." That's something for the vice president of the United States to call and ask you something like that. That's the way he was learning, by calling different people and asking what else he could do.

Libby recalls an event at the Governor's Mansion with John A. and how impressed she was with his clout and ability to talk to people.

> Libby: We went to the Governor's Mansion. I remember the time we drove up and we pulled up to the governor's yard, and he was making most of them park elsewhere. We drove up there and he said, 'Mr. Hobbs, go on in!' We drove on in to the Governor's Mansion; there weren't about eight or ten parking places up there. We parked there and the mayor of Nashville got out of his car, and the highway patrolman showed us where to park. We walked on over and gave our names to the Secret Service agent. He said, "Mr. Hobbs, step over here."

Vice President Al Gore with Libby and John A. Hobbs.

So, there was about a hundred twenty-five people in there, but they took us through the door and said, "The vice president is already here and doesn't want anybody to know it but you. He wants you upstairs in a few minutes, but we're waiting for him to call us and say it's okay to bring you up. We hate to ask you, but can we bring you through the kitchen and go up where they won't know you went up to stay?"

We went on upstairs, and I'll never forget Al Gore was coming down that long hall and he said, "Johnny and Libby! God, I want to talk to y'all, come on in here!" We went up where the governor lived on the top floor and went into the living room and sat down in there and we talked for at least thirty minutes. Johnny, the only thing I could think of was that I wish my mother and daddy could have seen me sitting with the vice president of the United States and us just talking. I was scared John, I didn't know what to say or what to do, but I tried to carry on a conversation. You and him just carried on and kidded and talked. Then Al Gore said, "I'm late, I better go on downstairs." He said, "I hate to ask y'all again to go through the kitchen, but all of those people are going to say, 'Why did Hobbs get up there and I didn't?'"

Governor Ned McWherter was a dear friend of John A.'s and helped him navigate tough political situations in Music Valley, especially when it came to large corporations against the "little guy." With Governor McWherter's assistance and backing, John A. was able to come out on top on more than one occasion.

When my good friend, Ned McWherter, first became the governor, he came out to eat dinner with us one day. I was having fried chicken, mashed potatoes, and everything he liked. We were all eating and he cussed like a sailor. Little Johnny was there, but only about sixteen years old. He said,

"Daddy, do all governors cuss like that?" I said, "That's just the way Ned is; he says what he thinks."

The highest compliment I've ever received came after Ned died. He was the forty-sixth governor of Tennessee and used to call and come out every now and then to visit. He even joined the Hooligans with us and would make sure that he sat next to me so we could talk. Louis and I really found that we had a friend in the Governor's Mansion who was willing to go to bat for us whenever we needed it the most in business. When he died from cancer in 2011, it was a tremendous loss and of course, I attended his funeral.

I was at a political function a few weeks later and Ned's son, Mike, came looking for me. He came over and he said, "I've been looking for you. I want to tell you, that you're the last man my daddy talked about. When he was laying in there dying and didn't have but a few minutes left, he said, "Tell Johnny Hobbs, I can't eat with him this week, I am afraid I won't be here." You're the last man he ever said anything about, and I knew you would want to know that."

John A. had friends from all backgrounds and occupations; they ranged from ditch diggers to judges, mayors, and governors, and on up. It didn't matter who you were or what you did, if you were his friend, you were his friend for life no matter what. Being nice to people and including them in your personal and business life was just plain smart.

CHAPTER THIRTY

Good Friends
and Great Causes

*There are three kinds of people in this world:
people who make it happen, people who watch what happens,
and people who wonder what happened.*
—TOMMY LASORDA

Sam Lovullo was *Hee Haw*'s only producer, which covered more than twenty years. *Hee Haw* was the show that replaced the Smothers Brothers Comedy Hour. *Hee Haw* opened to horrible reviews, but people watched it and within two months, everyone in America was watching *Hee Haw*. As the show became successful, Lovullo branched out and started doing different skits and shows such as the television series in the 1980s he called, *The Nashville Palace*. Sam named the series apparently without knowing there really was a club called The Nashville Palace, in Nashville, Tennessee owned by John A. One day after the taping, Ronnie Stoneman, who played the role of the ironing wife, Ida Lee Nagger on *Hee Haw,* told Lovullo she thought it was nice of him to make a skit for John A.'s "Palace." Lovullo, not knowing what Ronnie was talking about, asked her what she meant. She told him The Nashville Palace was owned by John A. Hobbs and

219

she thought the show was a tribute to his club. Since the show was already "in the can," Lovullo went to visit John A. personally and told him he'd taped a show called *The Nashville Palace*. He felt like he owed him both an apology and compensation for what he'd done without permission from John A. John A.'s response to the infraction was much more relaxed than Sam had anticipated and they became the best of friends ever since.

> For more than twenty years, Sam Lovullo worked with all the big stars on a show he created called *Hee Haw*. This was his variety television show featuring country western music and humor. Sam Lovullo came over to see me one time because he used my name for The Nashville Palace on his shows and thought I was going to sue him over it. He said, "Bud Wendell warned me that you were a good businessman. How much is this going to cost me? You've got us, because I did it without asking, but honestly, I didn't know you were over here."
>
> I laughed and I said, "Sam, sit down a minute."
>
> He said, "Okay."
>
> I asked him, "How much are you going to charge us? Tell your lawyers to draw up a paper and I don't want anything from you. Just keep using the name and help our business by plugging us often, and we'll help you in return."
>
> He looked surprised and said, "You don't want money out of it?" I said, "I don't want anything," and we became real close friends after that.

Former Los Angeles Dodgers Manager Tommy Lasorda and John A. became dear friends as well. Together, they would make the world so much better for a great number of people in need.

> That's the way me and Tommy became friends. The Los Angeles Dodgers had just won the World Series, and he came and sat at our table. People were sending over drinks

John A., Sam Lovullo, and Tommy Lasorda.

for us because we were sitting with him. We liked each other, and from that day on, we were really close friends for over forty years.

John A. reminisced about being together with Sam Lovullo and Tommy Lasorda and being caught in the middle of two very strong personalities.

Sam had come to town one time, and I was taking both Sam and Tommy to church on Sunday. I am driving and Tommy is with me, and we go by Sam's apartment and get him. When they both get in my car, they almost get in a fight every time. You've never ridden in a car until you get in the car with the two of them. Both of their personalities were ten feet tall.

We are headed to Saint Edward Catholic Church, and Tommy and Sam are arguing and got to battling back and forth about different people they knew.

I don't get in their argument, but said, "Here we're going to church and you two bastards are arguing before we even get in there!"

They laughed and stopped arguing for the moment and we walked into church. Father Joseph Breen asked, "Is that Tommy Lasorda?"

I said, "Yeah, and that's Sam Lovullo with the *Hee Haw* show."

He was very impressed and said, "Do you think Tommy might say something?"

I said, "Why don't you let him preach the sermon this morning? He'll do it, he's great!"

So, when it came time, Father Breen stopped the mass and said, "Johnny Hobbs has two celebrities with him today, Tommy Lasorda and Sam Lovullo. Tommy, I understand you almost became a minister at one time?"

Tommy nudged me and said, "You got me in this mess, didn't you?" Tommy went up to the altar and preached a good sermon about drug abuse. He had a ballplayer that got hooked on drugs and said that this kid could have been a super star, but drugs ate him up. He said, "All of you kids out in this church, remember drugs are the downfall of being an adult. You'll never go anywhere hooked on drugs."

John A. Hobbs is well known for a lot of things in his life, but most of all for his charitable contributions to important causes. There was no cause more important to him than that of the Catholic Church. Together with the help of now great friends, Tommy Lasorda and Sam Lovullo, a substantial sum of money was raised to build a convent for a special grammar school teacher and the Sisters of Mercy at Saint Bernard Convent.

I have done a lot of charity stuff in my life, but the one I am most proud of was the convent we built in 1989 for the Sisters of Mercy. These sisters have given their love and ministry to the Catholic Church in Tennessee since 1866. Mother Superior of the Saint Bernard Convent was my teacher in grammar school at Saint Ann's. Her name was Sister Mary Coleman, and I helped her a lot over the years. One day during a public speech, I said, "I want to introduce the Mother Superior, Sister Mary Coleman. She was my teacher in the fourth grade and she liked me so well, she kept me two years in a row!" She came to me for help when their convent was condemned and said that they needed a new home desperately.

Louis McRedmond and I met with the bishop and the board of directors, and they really didn't want to build a new convent until I finally got up to speak. "I want to tell all of you something. The sisters are living in a fire trap over there. Fifty nuns just got burned up over in England in a convent that wasn't fit to live in. If you don't build a new convent, you are going to regret it. Some of these sisters are in their nineties, and they can't get out of the building if something were to happen. If you don't build it, then let us build it. We'll raise the money, but it's just foolish to have those nuns living out there like that." The bishop finally admitted we were right, and told us that if we can raise the money, he will agree to let us build a new convent.

Knowing that Pennington Bend was a quiet country location, Louis McRedmond and I each paid a hundred fifty thousand dollars for land in the area and gave it to the nuns for their convent. Tommy, Sam, and I teamed up to contact people we knew to raise money through donations. SlimFast® and the owner of the Atlanta Hawks sent a substantial donation, and we had a gentleman that owned an airline send me thousands of dollars more. A couple of Los Angeles Dodgers baseball players offered Tommy thirty thousand dollars if he could lose 40 pounds. However if he didn't lose the 40 pounds he had to pay them the forty thousand dollars, instead.

I never will forget this. Tommy said, "Johnny, if you see I am not losing the weight after four weeks, hit me and break my jaw, then wire my mouth shut where I won't eat anything."

I said, "Ah hell, you can lose it." He got on SlimFast® and did an outstanding job losing that weight. I got a phone call one morning telling me to turn on my television. I turned it on and Lasorda was in New York talking about what he's going to do with the money when he loses the weight. He said, "I have a friend in Nashville, John A. Hobbs, and I want to donate it to the Catholic nuns for their new convent." He did an outstanding job of losing those pounds, and we added the money he earned to the growing donation pot.

Ralph Emery, John A., and Tommy Lasorda at Opryland Hotel.

We followed with a successful benefit held at the Grand Ole Opry house, called the *Grand Slam Variety Show.* Tommy and Sam packed the show with stars and it was a huge success. Pia Zadora loaned us her plane and pilot, never charging us for anything. Tommy brought in the entire Los Angeles Dodgers baseball team. This was the team that won the 1988 World Series against the Oakland Athletics. Superstars Robert Wagner and Elizabeth Taylor were on their way as well, but unfortunately, Ms. Taylor became ill mid-flight and had to continue on to her New York-based doctor. We had members of the *Hee Haw* show along with Irlene Mandrell, Minnie Pearl, Ralph Emery, Joe West, Ricky Van Shelton, Orel Hershiser, Boxcar Willie, George Lindsey, and so many more. I met the plane with a bus and transported everyone over to the show and provided the hotel rooms that night. In total, we raised about three hundred ninety thousand dollars for the project that year, which gave them a tremendous start. Then the following year we held a second benefit on the *General Jackson Showboat* and raised nearly a hundred thousand dollars more.

Sister Mary Coleman wrote John A. a special letter on December 8, 1989 to show her appreciation for all that he did.

December 8, 1989

Dear John:

Tommy Lasorda gave us much of his time and effort, and his generosity was beyond any expectation. All this brought us great happiness and help financially. We thank him! Indeed, we do thank him.

But, who brought us Tommy Lasorda? Today and forever, we will be grateful to you for your contact with Tommy and for so many things you have done for us.

Five years ago, after the fire warning was issued, you came to our rescue and you have never left us. Your name is not on a plaque, because you will not let it be, but it is engraved in the hearts of the Sisters of Mercy of Tennessee. The "Gala" was proclaimed by all as a spectacular event and the star was you, John Hobbs.

Yes, your "former" teacher (not "old" teacher) kept you two years in the fourth grade because she loved you so much and still does.

Gratefully,
Sister Mary Coleman, RSM

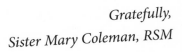

Sisters of Mercy Benefit Show at the Opry House..

John A. appreciated and respected the way Tommy worked with his fans, especially the children that would approach him for an autograph.

> When you were with Tommy, he would bring you down on the field and introduce you to all the players and stars. What I like most about Tommy is he makes kids say "Please." If a kid runs up to him and says, "Tommy, give me your autograph!" He'll say, "What's wrong with 'please'?" He'll make them say "please" first and then he will sign, trying to teach them a little bit. Tommy is one of the best in sports to give his autograph and help a lot of different people.

John A. loved to pick up the tab for large dinners out with his buddies, but he loved to watch them sweat even more, knowing that he would make it right later.

> Tommy Lasorda was up in Chicago playing the Cubs, so we traveled up there. That night we went out to eat with Major League Baseball umpire Joe West and all of our friends. When the waiter was bringing the check, I told the waiter to give it to the guy over there, and I pointed to our friend Charlie. He looked at the bill and put it down. Picked it up again and looked at it and then set it down. The guys started saying "Go ahead and pay for it." I said, "Don't say a word; let him pay for the damn thing and I'll give him the money later." So, it came to somewhere around seven hundred dollars and we let Charlie pay for it. The next night, he wouldn't even go out and eat with us; he went out to eat by himself.

Whenever John A. hosted Tommy in Nashville, the two of them seized every moment together. When it came time to return home, they both realized how much they truly appreciated each other and their strong friendship.

> Tommy still lives in a modest home outside of Anaheim, California. They have lived there for fifty years and his wife likes living there, so they have no plans to move. Last year they remodeled the home for the first time since they moved in. Tommy had both knees replaced in 1997 and his wife called me. She said, "Johnny, I am out on the front porch. Do me a favor, call Tommy back on his phone and talk him into flying to Nashville and staying with you for a few days. He's driving me crazy as hell out here." I waited about thirty minutes and called Tommy. He answered the phone and I said, "Hey! What the hell are you doing?"

He said, "Just sitting here bitching! Damn it, I've been in this bed long enough and I am getting up!"

I said, "Tommy, tell me what the hell has caused all of this excitement?"

He said, "Everything's going wrong."

"Why don't you fly out here and stay a week with me? You can stay here, and we'll go out and have a fun time."

He said, "I'd love it! I'll call the airport right now and hook me up a flight and call you back."

He called me back after a little while and said, "She's got me a flight," and told me what date and time he was coming in.

I went over to the airport to pick him up, and he was wearing those support hose all the way up his legs. I said, "Tommy, I never wore those things because they're not worth a damn. You just need support on the lower part. He said, "Alright." and he threw the things in the trash. Tommy stayed here about five days and seemed to enjoy himself. We went over to the convent to see the sisters we knew, went out to eat every day, and just messed around. He was in a happy mood when he left and joked, "Well, I am going back to the dungeon."

That day I carried him over to the airport, he said, "I was trying to think the other day. How long have you and I been friends?"

I said, "Tommy, let me see. You know it's close to forty-five years."

He said, "Damn it, time flies! Doesn't it? Well, we've been friends a long time, and I appreciate you."

There are so many stories to tell about good times and bending the rules. When Joe West was in the mix, life was always exciting. John A. has a great sense of humor and loves to set people up behind their back or pull a trick on them. Umpire Joe West was not immune from John A.'s shenanigans.

We had a large, deluxe show bus with real nice seats. Joe West said, "Pick us up in the morning from the hotel and all of us umpires will ride with you to the game." The next morning, they all come out and get on the bus, and while we were waiting out there for the game to start, the first baseman from one of the baseball teams came out and knocked on our bus door. We opened the door and I said, "Yeah?"

He said, "Whose bus is this?"

I said, "Umpire Joe West's."

"Damn, he's making a lot of money!"

I said, "Yeah, he's rich because he's made a lot of records."

So, we don't tell Joe about it and later when he was out there umpiring off of first base, the guy said, "Hey Ump! I saw your new bus out there. Boy, you sure have sold a lot of records to have that big bus."

Another time, we pulled up in front of the main gate at Wrigley Field, the Cubs' ballpark, and Joe showed his credentials. There was a young employee there manning the gate and he insisted that we couldn't park the bus there. He said, "You can't park here! You can't park here!"

Joe said, "Go tell your boss that there won't be any ballgame until we park this bus."

Well, out comes the vice president of the Cubs. He runs up to the bus and stops and says. "Oh, Joe! What are you doing?"

He said, "We need a place to park this bus."

He said, "Just put it up on the sidewalk."

We pulled up on the sidewalk, right in front of Cubs' Stadium (Wrigley Field), and parked the damn bus. Joe's a good guy to go out with, he's a lot of fun. He talks to everybody and we love that!

CHAPTER THIRTY-ONE

We Are All
in Your Corner

In the past, people were born royals.
Nowadays, royalty comes from what you do.
—PRINCESS DIANA

I f it is true that royalty comes from what you do during your life, then John A. Hobbs is undeniably a king. When The Nashville Palace closed after many legendary years, John A. and friends had nowhere to gather, and there was a noticeable

Building John A.'s Little Palace: Ronnie Hobbs, Joe Hobbs, and John A. Hobbs.

void in their lives and in Music Valley. The VFW and other local bars couldn't hold a candle to the atmosphere of The Nashville Palace, so he decided it was time to recreate it all on a smaller scale.

Utilizing a small lot he owned across the road from Fiddler's Inn North, he and his sons built John A.'s Little Palace in October 2005. Anxious to settle in there, a small group of about twenty-five friends and family celebrated the Fourth of July huddled at the construction site. The structure was framed with a roof and felt on it, and a few studs were strategically removed to allow entry. It started out hot that day, but the pouring rain brought relief and entertainment.

> We went down there on July the Fourth, and it was pouring down rain. We brought some sardines and everything. We set up a little bar inside where it was dry, but it was raining all around us. We had a big time. We all sat in there and partied and watched it rain.

When you are in the company of John A. and his family, the outward appearance and structure of people and places are unimportant. It is the people sharing time and space with them who matter the most. It is a bit like I can imagine heaven to be, void of levels and everyone is treated equally with love, friendship, and loyalty.

> I look back now and realize that I could talk to people and that made the biggest difference in my life. I never went by how important you were, or who you were; we were all just human. The mayor of Nashville came to a party at my place one time and he said, "John, I never have seen such a mix-up of people in my life. You have everybody from a ditch digger to a bank owner to the president of Opryland." I said, "Well,

they're all friends, and I never go by how much money you have. If I like you, I like you, and I don't care what you do. If you're a big star or whatever, I treat all alike. They're all good friends of mine, every last one of them."

Grand Ole Opry star Jeannie Seely is a dear friend of John A.'s and a regular who loves to come by John A.'s Restaurant after her Opry shows.

"I tell people all the time to be sure and make time to go to John A.'s. They'll say, 'What is John A.'s?' I'll say it's a neighborhood bar where you can go and relax and you know you have friends there. It's just a real friendly place. One of the most consistent things with John A.'s is that it helps you get off stage from the Opry. It's just a nice, friendly, clean, no fist fights, a little bit of bar atmosphere, a little bit of restaurant atmosphere, and nice place to take friends after the show. A good place for us to let down and let the adrenaline level out.

I never worry about introducing somebody to John A., because he always knows how to treat them and make them feel wonderful, whether they are the president of something or just somebody I went to school with a hundred years ago. He just knows how to treat people and we've all learned from him. The corner is his place and everybody respects it as that. He doesn't demand anything, it simply becomes that way because of the respect everybody has for him. It's a fair situation, because it gives everybody a place and a chance to spend a little time with him. He is absolutely the life of that corner. Otherwise it's just another place when he's not there."

As fate would have it, Marty Martel introduced me to John A. Hobbs and his corner of the world, nine years ago. I never fully realized this little corner contained such a strong social clique bound by decades of shared memories, loyal friendships, common interests, and a mutual respect for "the Man." I was welcomed into the corner almost immediately and remember being struck by John A.'s friendliness, warmth, hospitality, and remarkable stories. His appearance is common and down-to earth and the stories he shares without boast, so I truly had no knowledge of the depth of his wealth or vast array of seemingly superhuman accomplishments. I liked John A. for who he was in that corner and looking back, I am grateful that I had such little awareness of the extent of his awe back then.

In a world that is forever changing around us, this quaint club is one comfortable constant you can return to again and again. It is a place where you can relax and be yourself and where everything is in its place just as you remember it to be. The moment you pull open those glass doors, you feel like you did when you return home for the holidays. Smell of country food filling your senses and the thought of catfish and cornbread immediately make you salivate. You look to your left to see the bandstand with Dianne Sherrill or the house band performing your favorite classic country tune, and they always smile and wave. There are seated friends who stop you along the way and give you a hug, shake your hand, or pat you on the back with a sincere smile that says, "I am happy to see you here again."

Glancing to the back of the bar area, you can see the brim of John A.'s signature Greek fisherman's cap and hear Nancy Quinn's unmistakable voice. You make your way toward the corner, and before you even sit down, there is your "usual" drink waiting for you, thanks to bartender Tanya Brooks. John A. reaches out his hand and kisses you on the cheek. John A.'s special lady Nancy always smiles and says, "How you?" I love how she says that.

Nancy Quinn and John A.

John A. and Nancy lost their previous spouses to cancer, leaving a devastating void in their lives. As fate would have it, they ran into each other one night. As the conversation ensued, they began to reminisce about old friends and memorable times. After renewing their childhood friendship, they blossomed into a loving couple and close companions; you hardly ever see one without the other.

I never thought I'd be dating again at ninety years old.

Regular Carolyn McClain, can light up any room like a mason jar full of lightning bugs, and I always have to laugh every time I see the "special" glass she insists on drinking from while in the corner. Carolyn said:

"I can draw a little bit, and I've always wanted to draw that corner. It's in my head, back in that artistic part of my brain. I want to sketch it, and I believe I'll just do stick people and put them back there in the corner. The corner is always a crowd of stick people back there and you can't move. It's so funny, it's such a little corner and it's kind of strange back there in that corner, but it's the place to be. If you sit anywhere else, then you're just out of the loop. They may be good, bad whatever, but everybody in the corner is a character. I mean hell, that whole corner is a story. It's a story that probably can't be written because it is such a unique area. I don't know another spot in this town that has that."

Regular Ed Paschall, traditionally sits in the second bar stool down from John A. in the corner and is always impeccably dressed in his suit coat and slacks, with his gold money symbol ring on his wedding finger, drinking his usual vodka and diet tonic. The corner is cast with the colorful regulars that could be characters on a television sitcom. They are all vivid and memorable and soon you realize that you, too, are a character and that is why you fit in so well. I have heard it compared to *Cheers*, where everybody knows your name, what you drink, and most importantly where you sit. Some are in the corner out of habit, some out of need, some out of loneliness, and some just to be seen. Others are there to pay their respects to John A., to hear the stories and to have a good laugh or cry. I wouldn't want to leave anyone out, but if you have spent any time in the corner you know who the regular characters are. Like disc jockey and television host Keith Bilbrey says,

Bilbrey: You could do a sitcom in there. It's like the Nashville version of Cheers. You could almost match character for character on Cheers. We were over there this afternoon and John A. wasn't there, and it's just not the same feeling. I was sitting there watching one night, across from where he sits. I was just sitting there watching people come in and they always go back and pay homage to John A., and then before they leave, they've got to go back and say bye to John. It's

Joann Hobbs, Nancy Quinn, Sam Lovullo, Jack Kirby, and John A. in the corner of John A.'s Restaurant.

out of sheer respect, you know. I mean I wouldn't think of coming in here and not saying hi to John A., or coming back and saying bye to him as we leave. That's just the order of things. There's definitely a hierarchy in the corner, and I've always been honored to be part of that and to be recognized.

Although we have lost a few along the way, on any given weekend, the corner is still packed with friends and stars alike as it always has been. Stars such as Roy Clark, Jack Greene, Jeannie Seely, Jim Ed Brown, Jimmy C. Newman, Little Jimmy Dickens,

Roni Stoneman, and many, many more have frequented John A.'s after the Opry. John A.'s still keeps "The Wabash Cannonball" song alive and always requests a patriotic song, like his all-time favorite, "God Bless America." John A. plays host and usually buys drinks, appetizers, and cobblers for his friends in the corner, and it is such an honor to be offered the chance to get up on that stage and sing. All of your senses are engaged when you are sitting there. The sounds of the kitchen, clinking silverware from satisfied diners, laughter, classic country music, and the occasional "no peeking" alarm sounded from the ladies' room. You savor the taste of hot chicken and fried catfish, a cool drink and a unique dessert like deep fried MoonPies® all while listening to John A.'s guttural laughter. The sight of old and new friends, legendary entertainment on the stage, red curtains and American flags, pictures and memorabilia from sports figures, music legends and movie stars. The bar chair with a mind of its own twisting against your will, the warmth of the corner and the smell of country cooking. You just can't beat it!

My favorite place to sit in the corner is on the red bench seat facing out at the club. John A. is just to my right and the beer tap on the left. It is from this vantage point that you can witness what I like to call the court proceedings. John A. is king of this territory, and it is evident by the steady flow of people who traverse the chairs and characters to pay their respects. It's almost like a pilgrimage to see him. Some of the customers have been coming back for years and always make it a point to stop in and say hello. For some, it is their first time in Music Valley and they are curious to meet the owner they see in all the pictures surrounding their dinner tables.

I know somebody in almost every state and in every city, that has come into my place. I may not know their name right away, but when they remind me about what we did, then I can remember. I have people all of the time that come in and say, "Don't you remember me? Four years ago, I came in here from Atlanta and we sat in the corner and talked with So-and-so." Something like that and I would say, "Yeah!" Then it would dawn on me who they were. So many of them come back eight or ten years later, and I must meet a hundred people a day, and we get a lot of repeat business in here, which is what we like to see.

There is a hierarchy and protocol in seating and those that are closest to John A. know all of the unwritten rules to sitting in the corner. Mind you, these "rules" are not set forth by John A. himself, but by his friends out of sheer reverence for him. If you are sitting in the corner, you must be keenly aware of who joins the corner and make the necessary shift. The shift is in accordance to your place in this social hierarchy.

John A. sits at the head of the table, which I like to call the "Power Seat." It's the seat that we unconsciously designate to the one that has the most authority. Just to his right is Nancy Quinn in the "B1" position. The middle is for important guests, and I call my seat the "Gatekeeper." I can slide over at John A.'s nod and allow access to him, or I can stay steadfast in my position limiting the conversation and contact. If a star, judge, or long-time friend comes in, I know my seat is trumped, and I willingly move down.

There is definitely a shift in the seating dynamics when John A. and Nancy come in for the evening. The first table in front of John A. is usually filled with his closest friends, Ed Paschall always has his chair at the bar near John A., and then we trickle down to the last table at the end of the row. It always amazes me that even when John A. is not there, his seat will remain vacant. It can be standing room only and that one seat will still be left open. Now that's respect! There is usually a reserve sign on the first couple of tables in the corner, but truly it isn't necessary because most everyone knows the protocol.

Star studded birthday bash—Roni Stoneman, Jim Ed Brown, Helen Cornelius, Jeannie Seely, Jan Howard, Jimmy C. Newman, and Johnny Counterfit.

When John A. is not there at the club, there is a different energy and friends won't come in or stay long without him there. He is the life of the party and the reason we all like to be there. Honestly, I think we need a flag with a Greek fisherman's cap on it flying high atop the restaurant to let us all know when John A. is there. Much like the Queen of England has when she is in residence at her palace and the Royal Standard of the United Kingdom is flown. At John A.'s we don't have a flag, only his silver minivan to look for. If it is parked just out front of the main door, then you know he is there and it will be a fun night.

John A.'s is truly a little palace in a kingdom with a worthy king, loyal subjects, a vast territory and a law by which it is governed. "In short there's simply not, a more congenial spot, for happily-ever-aftering than here in… Music Valley." —*from Richard Burton Camelot Lyrics.*

CHAPTER THIRTY-TWO

Lengthening Shadows

The shadows are lengthening for me. The twilight is here.
My days of old have vanished—tone and tint.
They have gone glimmering through the dreams of things that were.
Their memory is one of wondrous beauty, watered by tears
and coaxed and caressed by the smiles of yesterday.
—GENERAL DOUGLAS MACARTHUR

had a lot of friends to help me everywhere. I learned so much from people that I could use in my lifetime. Our business was lucky enough. Not to have but an eighth grade education, I was very lucky. I am glad that all my boys are hard workers, too.

Ronnie doubled the size of the Scoreboard Bar and Grill. So, all my boys went down there and nailed sheet. My grandsons were up there, all of them on the roof, and they all worked hard. It made me feel good when I rode by and saw them all up there driving nails and working together. I trained them in the business. My boys would rather give to somebody than take something, and I am proud of them. I am proud of what they do and what they did in business.

They're increasing the businesses, they're making them bigger and better. They're doing pretty damn good. Those boys built the business up, they worked hard and now they have it where they can rest a little bit. I would never have succeeded the way I did in my life without the help of my children. They made it all possible, and I am so grateful to them all.

At one time Music Valley was the most popular place in Nashville and it will come back. You have to go back years ago, when The Nashville Palace and the Stock-Yard were the only two places going in Nashville. You either went there or you didn't go out at all. Music Valley's going to keep growing. There'll be something big to come out here again one day because Opryland wants something great.

Joe Hobbs, John A., Ronnie Hobbs, and Johnny C. Hobbs.

Times are changing and the public has to change by what I've seen in just my short lifetime, seems like a long time, but it's really short. The years roll by and times are changing really fast. I look back on most of the Opry stars and they are dead now. We lost 'Tater' and so many of the main, old stars, all of which were such good friends. We just lost the Cajun, Jimmy C. Newman, and Jim Ed Brown before that.

You know what Jimmy C. Newman did about two months before he died? I was sitting in the corner at my restaurant about nine-thirty at night, and I looked up and saw him coming through the door. He came on back to the corner and said, "I just wanted to stop by and talk to you a minute. I want you to know that I haven't been coming over to see you because I can't drive after dark. I got Miss May out in the car, and I told her that I wanted to come in and tell you why I haven't been out here. I didn't want you to get mad at me. We're going to stay down here tonight instead of driving back to Murfreesboro, but I just wanted to talk to you and tell you that I will be back by to see you." That was the last time we saw each other, but he was a good man and a dear friend.

During our final interview, I made the comment, "You sure have lost a lot of friends, John A." He sat back in his chair and said:

Yeah, Lord God, I guess that's what happens when you get old. They all start dropping. I am afraid of dying. I am just afraid because I don't know where I am going and if it's really a place. I read what Saint Mother Teresa said. She didn't know whether there was a heaven or hell or anything after this earth. I thought, "If a saint wonders, then I know I'll wonder about it." We didn't know anything before we came in, we may go out the same way.

I reflected for a moment and added, "I'd like to think there's something else, John."

> I do, too. I was taught that and I believe it, but still I have a little doubt. There's so many unanswered questions. I don't believe there's streets of gold and pearly gates and all of that. I don't believe you'll know anybody up there. I think when you get up there it will be all new; people will be happy. I believe that everybody will be happy and it's a place to enjoy and evidently you don't need food or anything. I used to be scared to death when I'd die. Then I watched so many people die, like my mother, Libby, and all these people I knew have died. I thought, "Well, if they can go through it, I can, too." I look at a frail little lady and I think, "If she can go up there, I know I can." So, whatever happens, there's no way out of it, everyone dies."
>
> That's the main thing, I hate to leave my family. That's the only thing I really dread. You know, me and the boys are real close. We see each other every day and all throughout our lives, we've seen each other every day. We plan business and work business together. You've got to remember now, Mike is sixty-nine, Joe is sixty-six, Ronnie's sixty-four, and Johnny, he's fifty-three. One thing I pray for is this: I don't want anything to happen to my kids. I tell God all the time, "If you're going to take somebody, take me, don't take them." One thing, nobody knows what happens, nobody's come back, and nobody has given us a signal that they were there. I don't understand when I hear people say they've seen a ghost. I don't believe any of that. I do know that the closer you get to death, the more you think about it.

I was thinking of all the awards John A. has received in his lifetime from humanitarian awards to highway dedications and all the places he built and owned along the way. I was so sure what the answer to my next question would be, but I asked John A. anyway. I asked, "When all is said, and done, what do you want to be remembered most for, John?" He didn't hesitate for even a second before answering me this:

> That I was a good friend and if they needed help, I was there. I've helped a lot of friends in a lot of ways. With money and in a lot of other ways, but I do what I can for people. Also, that I treated everybody fair, the best I knew how, and I was honest with everybody. That's all I want. I stayed friends with most of them, and there is no such thing as a self-made man. Without a lot of help and friends, nobody can make it in this world.

John A.'s answer surprised me, but then I was immediately hit with the enlightenment of it all. It was so selfless, so simple, and yet so profound. I admit that I felt a little ashamed that I had placed so much emphasis in my mind on accolades and material achievements. John A. gave me the greatest lesson of my life and I realized exactly what the "Golden Thread" of his book would be. I smiled, turned off the recorder, and just sat in awe of the man before me.

John A. and author, Julie Richardson, in the corner, 2016.

Afterword

In this world, you will have to make your own way.
To do that, you must have friends. You can make friends
by being honest, and you can keep them by being steadfast.
You must keep in mind that friends worth having
will in the long run expect as much from you as they give to you.

—ELIZABETH HUTCHINSON
(President Andrew Jackson's mother)

I have spent the last forty-five years of my life thinking that the secret to happiness is an abundance of material resources. I have amassed many things like my beautiful home, reliable transportation, convenient modes of communication, walk-in closets packed with clothes, expensive jewelry, collectibles, and the list continues. I have so much and yet, I felt as if it had me. To maintain it all, I relentlessly chased life as it pulled me one way and then the other, up and then down.

I am running as fast as I can, always pushing to accomplish more, to have more, do more, and to be more. There is never a finish line, and, apparently, I am addicted to the race. Life for me is as if I am on a moving walkway, passing others along the way, increasing my speed with each defining moment in my life.

Writing this book was no doubt one of my greatest accomplishments, but I never realized the effect the process would have on me. Here I was trying to do something exceptional for John A. and his family, and ended up getting the most incredible gift in return. The hours of personal conversations with Mr. Hobbs offered me qualitative lessons about life that shattered my perceptions. I learned life *is* about accomplishing great things, affluence, and abundance. It *is* about adventure, embracing change and taking risks. However, all of this is made possible through family, friendship, and love. You must have a lot of help along your journey and in turn you must be there for others and always make a positive contribution to society.

Finishing this book for me was like coming to the end of that moving walkway I was on. When I finally stepped off, there was this feeling of a little lag in my forward motion as I stumbled a step until I slowed to match the natural cadence of life.

It feels a little strange at first, but now life is more in focus and more enjoyable. I still have quantity, but now I am focused on quality and it has changed my life forever.

Mr. Hobbs: Thank you for your life and for the priceless lessons you have so graciously shared with me, and the world. You truly are my hero, and I am eternally grateful for your trust and belief in me. You have been loved by so many in this world, and I am grateful to be one of them. Thanks to you, I am no longer worried about being the most interesting person in the room. I just want to be the most cherished person in the room, like you.

Notes

[1] Barker, Gary, Broster, John B. *The Johnson Site* (40Dv400): *A Dated Paleoindian and Early Archaic Occupation in Tennessee's Central Basin*: Journal of Alabama Archaeology, 1996, p. 97-153.

[2] Deter-Wolf, Aaron, Peres, Tanya M., *Recent Research in the Middle Cumberland River Valley*: Introduction to the Special Volume, Tennessee Archaeology, 2012, p. 5-17.

[3] Nipper, Skip, *Salt and Sulphur*, 262 Down Right: Stories of Sulphur Dell and Baseball, 2013.

[4] Bucy, Carol. *Nashville's Historical Timeline*, Metropolitan Nashville Historical Commission, 2015.

[5] Simpson-Arnow, Harriette, Ripley-Wolf, Margaret. *Flowering of the Cumberland*, Michigan State University, 984, p. 10-11.

[6] Creighton, Wilbur, Johnson, Leland R. *Building of Nashville*, Self-Published, Tennessee, 1969.

[7] Durham, Walter T. *Nashville: The Occupied City 1862-1863*, University of Tennessee Press, 2008.

[8] U.S. Census Bureau Data for 50 Largest Cities, 1850-1990, *www.census.gov*

[9] Nashville-Davidson County, Tennessee 1928 Weather History *www.usclimatedata.com*

[10] Millman, Dan. *The Life You Were Born to Live*, Tiburon, California, H.J. Kramer Inc., 1993 p. 230-236.

[11] Kyvig, David E. *Daily Life in the United States, 1920-1940: How Americans Lived Through the Roaring Twenties and the Great Depression*, Chicago, Ivan R. Dee, 2002.

[12] Arnesen, Eric, *Encyclopedia of U.S. Labor and Working-Class History*, New York: Rutledge, 2007, P. 154

[13] Tennessee Department of Corrections, *Tennessee State Penitentiary*, *www.tn.gov*, 2009.

[14] Tyner, James A. *War and Violence, and Population: Making the Body Count*, Guilford Press 1st Edition, Sommerville, 2008 p. 5/Axelrod, Alan. *Encyclopedia of World War II*, Volume 1, Info Base Publishing, 2001 p. 659

[15] Rozeff, Norman. *Army Airman in Sailor's Hats*, 1991, *www.navymemoryshop.com/airplanesupportgeneral-Lyon.html*.

[16] Wow Philippines: Palawan: *The Philippines' Last Frontier*, Way Back Machine, 2008/US Cruisers List: *Light/Heavy/ Antiaircraft Cruisers*, Part 1, *www.hazegray.org*, 2000.

[17] Manchester, William. *American Caesar: Douglas MacArthur 1880-1964*, Little, Brown 2008, p. 179.

[18] Bernstein, Barton J. *The Uneasy Alliance: Roosevelt, Churchill, and the Atomic Bomb, 1940-1945*, The Western Political Quarterly, University of Utah Press, 1976, p. 202-230.

[19] Comancho, Benito. *Bockscar, History, War and Weapons*, Thor, 2010.

[20] History.com, Staff, *Bombing of Hiroshima and Nagasaki*, A & E Networks, 2009.

[21] Murphy, Kevin C. *Inside the Bataan Death March: Defeat, Travail and Memory*. Jefferson, North Carolina: McFarland, 2014.

[22] Adamson, Hans Christian, Kosco, George Francis. *Halsey's Typhoons: A Firsthand Account of How Two Typhoons, More Powerful Than the Japanese, Dealt Death and Destruction to Admiral Halsey's Third Fleet*, New York: Crown Publishers, 1967.

[23] Biography.com Editors, *Jack Johnson Biography*, A & E Networks, 2017.

[24] Rudy, Jannette C. *A Bend in the Cumberland*, Favorite Recipes: Nashville, Tennessee, 1991, p. 25-30, 36-38, 40-60, 159, 168-170, 175.

[25] Phillips, J.T. *The Tennessean, History of the Opryland Theme Park*, 2016.

[26] Murrells, Joseph, *The Book of Golden Discs* 2nd Edition, London: Barrie and Jenkins Ltd., 1978, p. 61.

[27] Mansfield, Brian, Erlewine, Stephen Thomas. *Randy Travis Biography*. All Music 2011.

[28] *www.rickyvanshelton.com*

[29] Hall, Wade. *Hell-Bent for Music: The Life of Pee Wee King*, University Press of Kentucky, 1996, p. 146-147.

[30] Trott, Walt. *Boxcar Willie, Encyclopedia of Country Music*, New York: Oxford University Press, 1998, p. 47.

[31] *www.Boxcarwillie.com/biography.php.*

[32] Zwisohn, Laurence. *Happy Trails: The Life of Roy Rogers*, 2014. *www.royrogers.com*

[33] Autry, Gene. *Back in the Saddle Again*, New York: Doubleday, 1978.

[34] Phillips, J.T. *The Tennessean, History of the Opryland Theme Park*, 2016.

About the Author

Alana Rothstein

Julie Richardson is a Colorado native and lives in Golden, CO. She earned her degree from the University of Colorado at Boulder. Her background is multifarious with teaching, business ownership, travel, and professional singing. In 2008, Richardson moved to Nashville to pursue her music career. Her manager at the time, Marty Martel introduced her to "The Corner," where John A. Hobbs holds court as the Godfather of Music Valley. Her friendship, admiration, and sincere interest in the life and times of John A. Hobbs moved her to write this biography/ memoir. The words nestled on these pages pass on a history and legend that should never be forgotten. Richardson is honored to play a part in preserving it for generations to come.

Contact Julie Richardson via e-mail at *waitinthetruck@msn.com*, visit her website at *www.JulieRichardsonMusic.com*.

Additional copies can be purchased at *www.JAHobbs.com* or by contacting the publisher directly.

"*That I was a good friend and if they needed help, I was there.*"
—John A. Hobbs, 2016